REWARDING RETIREMENT

BRIAN D. ALLEN, CFP®

REWARDING RETIREMENT

HOW FIDUCIARY COMMITTEES CAN ELEVATE WORKERS, COMPANIES, AND COMMUNITIES

Published by Advantage, Charleston, South Carolina.
Member of Advantage Media Group.

ADVANTAGE is a registered trademark, and the Advantage colophon is a trademark of Advantage Media Group, Inc.

Printed in the United States of America.

10 9 8 7 6 5 4 3 2 1

ISBN: 978-1-64225-146-3
LCCN: 2020909493

Cover design by David Taylor.
Layout design by Carly Blake.

Advantage Media Group is proud to be a part of the Tree Neutral® program. Tree Neutral offsets the number of trees consumed in the production and printing of this book by taking proactive steps such as planting trees in direct proportion to the number of trees used to print books. To learn more about Tree Neutral, please visit **www.treeneutral.com**.

"Do to others as you would have them do to you."

—Luke 6:31 (NIV)

CONTENTS

INTRODUCTION

AN HONOR AND A CHALLENGE

At critical times in our lives, we count on others. We rely on medical professionals to take good care of us. In emergencies we rely on police, firefighters, and other first responders. Legal issues? We look for a good attorney. Time after time, we depend on those whose jobs are to put us first. These are the people who keep us healthy, safe, and secure.

Looking out for our financial security is another group of committed souls who are virtually never in the limelight but who nonetheless play a critical role. Across the nation, at companies and nonprofits small and large, countless individuals serve on committees that oversee the 401(k) and 403(b) plans on which most Americans today base their retirement dreams. The vigilance of those committees is critical in this post-pension era in which employees must determine how much to accumulate for their retirement and try their hand at the investments that companies once undertook on their behalf.

It is for those dedicated servants that I write this book—and because you are reading it, you likely are one of them. The United States has hundreds of thousands of these employer-sponsored retirement plans, which means that millions of people like you have taken a turn as a committee member.[1] Your mission is to look out solely for the best interests of your colleagues, who tuck away their hard-earned pay, week after week, year after year. Yes, you are helping your organization, too, by ensuring that it is offering an attractive and effective retirement plan, but helping the boss is not why you have been chosen for this role. Your foremost duty is to do what is best for the participants, above anyone else. You are a true fiduciary.

Serving on a fiduciary committee is a sobering responsibility. Your coworkers are counting on your good judgment and skills to ensure their retirement success. Their spouses and families are relying on you too. If you do a poor job, people will get hurt. When people get hurt, they often look for something or someone to blame—and you will become very aware of the pitfalls of doing a bad job. Much industry news has focused on what those hurt people do to get even, and the media have been quick to report on a flood of litigation.

As a result, many fiduciary committees take a protective stance rather than a progressive one. When they meet, they devote much of their time to the topic of how to fend off lawsuits—an understandable perspective, perhaps, but unfortunate. Think of it this way: would you want your doctor to focus on how to keep you in the best of health or on whatever it takes to keep you from filing a lawsuit? The latter

1 "Private Pension Plan Bulletin: Abstract of 2016 Form 5500 Annual Reports," DOL Employee Benefits Security Administration, December 2018.

is not most people's idea of preventive medicine. Likewise, a good teacher concentrates on challenging every pupil, not on appeasing every parent. A well-trained police officer uses handcuffs, not just kid gloves. Should professionals be aware of potential legal issues? Yes. Obsessed with them? No.

Fiduciary committee members, when they are at their best, focus on those whom they serve, the plan's participants. If you do your job well, people will benefit in many ways. By helping individuals and their families, you also are improving communities, and better communities make for a better nation. In short, you are doing your part to build a stronger society, which is a supremely rewarding endeavor. That's not a job for the timid. Sure, you need to avoid trouble, and this book will teach you how. More importantly, however, this book will show you how to know that you are doing your job well.

No need to guess. As a member of a fiduciary committee, you can be confident that you are keeping your commitment to assure your colleagues of a good retirement plan. In the chapters ahead, I will outline three tests that committees can use to measure and quantify whether a plan is performing well. Until now, many just didn't know. They based their assessments on the opinions of their advisers and consultants, who told them just what you might expect. Those advisers were not inclined to say, "Hey, we've been doing a terrible job for you here, folks, so you'd better look for someone else!"

When you have finished this book, you no longer will be in the dark when it comes to what is terrible and what is terrific. I will explain specifically what I believe constitutes a good plan so that those involved in its operation do not need to wonder whether they have succeeded. I will lay out for you key measurements needed to accurately assess the quality of a plan.

With a few exceptions that I will explain, the tools and tips in this book apply both to the 401(k)—the type of plan that serves employees in the private, for-profit world—and the 403(b), which serves certain employees of nonprofits. In this book, I will refer to them collectively as "retirement plans," with the understanding that I am not referring to the old-style, defined-benefit pension plans, which the defined-contribution plans largely have replaced since the 1980s. For both 401(k) and 403(b) plans, I will be assuming that these plans are subject to the general provisions of the Employee Retirement Income Security Act (ERISA). Not all plans are subject to ERISA. Much of this book will not apply to these exempt plans.

Throughout, I will emphasize the honor and privilege of your role on a fiduciary committee. Yes, your responsibility is a serious one and caution is always wise—but remember that the mission of any good plan is to help people attain a fulfilling retirement. You should proceed not in fear of doing something wrong but instead determined to do it right—and to do right. You have been chosen to help your colleagues prosper in life. Your duty is to look out for them. If you keep that top of mind, and if you remain focused on my three tests of a retirement plan's excellence, the risks that come from doing a poor job will largely melt away.

A PLACE OF CONFIDENCE

Your role as a retirement plan committee member is a significant one. You have been entrusted to help provide employees with a good plan, one that successfully prepares them for retirement. As you oversee the management of the plan, the decisions that you and your fellow members make will impact its expenses and the investment choices offered. The service providers you choose will have much to do with how well or how poorly the plan is run.

As a fiduciary, you have personal and legal responsibilities to make reasonable decisions on behalf of everyone who participates in the plan and their beneficiaries. It is your duty to make all decisions with their best interests in mind. That is the essence of being a fiduciary. It is considered the highest standard of care under the law. Fiduciaries are required to put the interests of those they serve ahead of their own.

You have been entrusted to help provide employees with a good plan, one that successfully prepares them for retirement.

In recent years, more people than ever have become familiar with the fiduciary concept: it became a frequent topic of news reports with the coming and going of the Department of Labor's Fiduciary Rule, which would have significantly influenced the operation of retirement plans. In early 2017, the government began phasing in the long-debated rule, which expanded the fiduciary standard to anyone, including representatives of brokerages and insurance companies, who offered investment advice to plan sponsors and participants. The Fiduciary Rule was one of the most hotly debated topics in finance, with many brokers and investment firms doing all they could to halt it from being enacted. Seeking to hold all retirement plan investment advisers accountable, the regulation was expected to impact those that sold products for commissions the most. With the changing of the political guard, however, the Fiduciary Rule quickly fell out of favor, and by the spring of 2018 it was dead. A federal court ruled that the Department of Labor had overreached its authority.

Despite the demise of the Fiduciary Rule, the publicity that it generated served to raise public awareness of the fact that not all plan advisers are equal—that is, they are not necessarily fiduciaries. Before the Fiduciary Rule, many advisers needed only suggest suitable investments, which very well could suit themselves, too, in the form of big commissions. If the new rule had stood, it would have eliminated many commission structures that define the industry.

For the record, I am a fiduciary. My company, Pension Consultants Inc., which I founded in 1994, operates solely under that standard. We are what is known as a 3(38) fiduciary with discretion to manage the investment lineups in our clients' plans. In effect, those clients transfer to us the responsibility to serve the participants' best interests. More on that in chapter 5, which will examine the varying roles of plan advisers and what you, as a fiduciary committee member, should consider in evaluating your teammates.

In your role as a fiduciary, you may be experiencing feelings of both pride and hesitancy. Of course, you want to do a good job, but at this point you probably are unsure how to do that or even how you would know. This is unfamiliar territory. You find yourself on a committee that consists, typically, of five to a dozen members. Some are serving by virtue of their title—your organization's chief financial officer, for example, or the director of human resources, or the director of benefits. The presumption is that those executives have the background and knowledge to serve the committee well, though their allegiance to the employer must never stand in the way of their duty to put the plan's participants' interests first. Others have been chosen to serve because of their long tenure or senior position, or perhaps they simply are known around the office to have an interest in finances and investments.

Most feel honored to be appointed, but many quickly begin to feel as if they are in over their heads. The legal and investment lingo can feel intimidating to the uninitiated. As a newbie on a committee, you likely will hear words that are unfamiliar to you and conclude that your colleagues know a lot more than you do. Perhaps some do, but that doesn't mean that they are smarter or better suited to serve than you. You also likely will hear a lot of talk about the risks of non-compliance and daunting descriptions of things that can go wrong if everything isn't done to the letter. You may begin to doubt whether you should be in this role.

At such times, remember again why you are serving. You have been chosen for a reason—to see that everyone involved, including each of your fellow committee members, keeps the focus squarely on serving the best interests of the participants. Your duty is to provide a good retirement plan for them that can make a profound difference in the quality of their lives. You should take pride in that role. Even if you don't yet know the lingo or all the protocol, you certainly can ask the right questions to ensure that everyone is playing by the rules. I am writing this book so you can know what those questions should be.

Whether your committee has a formal or informal structure, and no matter how often it meets, it is imperative that you pay close attention. A few organizations, generally those that sponsor larger plans with over $1 billion in assets, divide the responsibilities into two committees, one to oversee the investment lineup and the other to oversee compliance. Most organizations, though, have one committee that deals with both, and I have written this book from that perspective. Either way, you still are a fiduciary. You are an advocate for your fellow employees, and it is your duty and privilege to remain vigilant and to speak up on their behalf during meetings.

Your voice matters. These chapters will help you to fill in the blanks in your knowledge so that you can contribute meaningfully to the proceedings. Often, newly appointed fiduciaries don't feel that they belong until they have served two or three years. What you will learn in this book will help get you up to speed much sooner. In short, my goal is to take you from a place of uncertainty to a place of confidence.

A DIFFERENT APPROACH

By and large, whether a retirement plan is good or bad has been anyone's guess. In my three decades in this industry, I have often observed how investment advisers and managers have benefited from that subjective assessment. Let's say a manager proudly informed you that one of your investments made a 10 percent return last year. Sound good? Now suppose you could have bought into an index fund and earned 16 percent. Still happy? Because of a lack of transparency, too many investment advisers and managers have been able to spin their poor performance to give the impression that they are shining. The unsophisticated consumers of their advice are mostly left to judge their competence on their personality, not their actual value.

That has been the case in many industries and professions. For example, if you ask most patients whether they have a good doctor, my guess is that they will say they do. Why? Because the doctor listens to them and explains things carefully—and those are good traits in a doctor, for sure. What gets lost, however, is that the true value of a doctor is to diagnose injuries and disease and to prescribe the right treatments. Because patients lack objective information on the doctor's performance, they base their assessment on personality and image.

In this age of big data, however, that is changing. Poor performers are finding it increasingly difficult to hide. Transparency is becoming the norm in our society, and professionals can either resist that change or welcome it. It's easy to see why some would resist, but the better performers have nothing to fear. To remove a cloak of confusion should be good for all concerned—and it is good business too. In my industry, the data shine a light on just how well a retirement plan is performing. You can take precise measurements: it's either a good plan, or it's not. The greater transparency promotes objectivity—and that is the approach that my company has chosen to embrace.

My colleagues and I are privileged to be at the forefront of this new way of looking at the retirement plans that are bringing financial freedom to countless Americans. The business world has long intrigued me. I enjoy the teamwork of putting together a successful enterprise, knowing that "we made this." I also enjoy the complexity of economics and the markets, which have fascinated me since my high school days. At Pension Consultants, where our mission is to improve the financial security of American workers, I consider what we have made to be more than a business. It's a calling. All those people and their families are counting on us to take good care of them, and we must not let them down.

CHAPTER 1

GOOD FOR ONE AND ALL

Meet Karen.[2]

Karen is thirty-six years old and works the evening shift at a hospital as a nurse's assistant. Her husband works days as an inside sales rep for a plumbing supply company. They have two preteen kids. Most of the time, they have enough money to get by, but they still live paycheck to paycheck—and if either of them misses one of those checks, the family struggles.

When there isn't enough in the bank account to make ends meet, or to pay for extras like sports fees and birthday parties, Karen and her husband rely on a couple of credit cards. They had expected to use

2 The hypothetical scenario does not represent specific facts and is intended to illustrate general financial issues relating to participants of company sponsored retirement plans. It is in no way meant to be an endorsement of PCI as an investment adviser or a testimonial about PCI clients' actual experiences with PCI as an investment adviser.

them only for emergencies, but it didn't work out that way. Typically, one of the cards is maxed out and the other is nearly so. They always intend to pay them down, but the money never seems to stretch that far. Instead, they manage each month to pay off just enough to use one of them a little longer.

Karen and her husband both have hoped to start saving for retirement. A couple of times, they have come close. Once, with retirement in mind, they even set aside a thousand dollars from a tax refund and put it into their credit union account. But some pressing concern always comes along, and those savings evaporate as they turn their attention back to the here and now. Karen worries sometimes about how they ever will manage to retire, but her anxiety about tomorrow takes a backseat to her anxieties of today. Almost every week, she gets a reminder of the precarious position that her family is in. The dryer goes on the blink. One of the children needs to see the doctor. Yet another school expense crops up. For months, she has noticed that her car's tires are getting bald, but those other expenses keep getting in the way. Something, always something.

When she and her husband manage to cross paths for a few minutes each day, it seems that money troubles and overdue bills are all they talk about anymore, if they talk at all. Karen wonders what kind of example they must be setting for the kids, who can feel the brooding tension in the household. She finds herself snapping at them over next to nothing. Not only are her family relationships suffering, her work is suffering too. Instead of giving her full attention to her job, she spends time dealing with whatever emergency has come her way that day—and the boss has noticed how distracted she seems.

Karen feels as though her financial future is out of her control. With all that constant stress over finances, she feels like a failure. She fears that instead of enjoying a storybook retirement, she and her husband will have to keep on working just to pay the bills.

One important protection against financial insecurity is an employer-sponsored retirement plan. To accumulate wealth requires discipline, and people who are inclined to overspend will do so whether they make $40,000 a year or $400,000 a year. You can never become wealthy if you spend more than you make—and for many people, a retirement plan makes all the difference, because it forces the discipline of saving.

A GOOD PLAN SERVES THE EMPLOYEES

What is the purpose of a retirement plan? Employers offer retirement plans as a benefit to their employees, allowing them to build financial security and preparing them to retire successfully. That sense of security can make a world of difference for those employees and their families.

Let's go back to Karen's story.

Tired of the anxiety and determined to move her family into a position of financial security, she decides to enroll in her hospital's 403(b) retirement plan. To her surprise, she doesn't really notice the money that has been diverted from the family's day-to-day budget. She selected the traditional pretax option, so her contributions come out before taxes and before she even receives her paycheck. Her employer matches her contributions as part of the plan structure, and before long she has $3,000 saved in her account. Karen understands that she shouldn't withdraw the money, but just knowing it's there gives her a feeling of success and security. For the first time in her life, she can see a financial future.

Buoyed by their increased feelings of control, she and her husband decide to begin an emergency savings account, using an automatic payroll deduction plan that her employer provides. Once again, the money is deducted before the paychecks are deposited in the bank, and the money seems to accumulate quickly and painlessly.

Because her anxiety has eased, Karen becomes less distracted and more reliable at work, and her improved performance catches her manager's attention. Eventually, she gets more responsibility and an increase in pay. Feeling increasingly confident, the couple dedicate that increase to improving their financial situation even more. Karen's relationships with her children become less strained as she feels reassured that she can provide for them.

From what I have observed over my career, many people experience a similar change of heart once they succeed in saving for the future. A feeling of improved financial security can alleviate a major source of stress that employees carry with them into the workplace. With less worry on their minds, they can perform at their best levels. This improved performance could lead to enhanced career growth, higher income, and an overall improved quality of life.

Additionally, success in building financial security for retirement can translate to other aspects of employees' financial life. Increased confidence in their financial planning skills can lead them to further accomplishments, including keeping debt under control, saving for their kids' college expenses, and accomplishing long-term financial goals.

A GOOD PLAN SERVES THE EMPLOYER

When the employees are happy, so is the employer—and that is because employees' relief from financial stress can dramatically increase their productivity and the fortunes of the organization. It only makes sense. If you are worried about your car getting repossessed or making the mortgage, are you likely to be performing at your best?

That anxiety, multiplied by the millions who are feeling it, comes at a high cost to our society. Distracted workers not only make less money for themselves but less for their employers too. A study by the consulting firm Mercer pegged the cost of worker insecurity at $250 billion annually in terms of lost productivity.[3] Good retirement plans can go far in reversing that damage. As employees see their accounts growing, they feel a greater focus and dedication to the job that has made those savings possible.

When the employees are happy, so is the employer.

On many levels, employers benefit from offering their workers a superior retirement plan. In today's competitive marketplace, where companies often compete for top employees, an excellent plan could become a differentiator in the company's efforts to attract and retain the best people. The cost of employee turnover can be high, and a quality retirement plan could serve as a key part of an attractive overall compensation and benefits package.

In addition, an organization with a well-functioning plan will gain the assurance that its employees will be able to retire on time. Obviously that is good for them, but consider the impact on the organization. Employees who are in their sixties tend to be the more highly compensated ones. When they leave their jobs voluntarily to begin a comfortable retirement, they open positions in the workforce for replacements who are younger—and who will start out lower on the pay scale.

That benefits employers in two ways. They are bringing aboard ambitious new hires who tend to have the progressive ideas and fresh perspectives that are the hallmark of youth. Retiring workers open

3 "Financial Stress Could Cost Employers up to $250 Billion Annually," *Think Advisor*, August 24, 2017, https://www.thinkadvisor.com/2017/08/24/financial-stress-could-cost-employers-up-to-250b-i/.

up advancement opportunities for younger workers. This allows younger workers to stay longer with the company as they envision a future of challenge and opportunity. Their contributions will keep the company relevant and thriving. And the immediate cost savings can be significant. Let's say that Sam, who is retiring, earned $85,000 a year. In comes Deidra to replace him, making $65,000 a year. That is an immediate savings of $20,000 annually for that one position. Multiply that amount by the hundreds of people who come and go in a large company, and you can see the huge advantage to the bottom line of having a plan that gives employees the financial confidence to proceed into retirement.

Sometimes, CFOs can miss these long-term savings to the company. Increased worker productivity and lower compensation costs from retirements are real, but they don't show up right away. A CFO will instinctively understand that attracting more participants in the plan will mean higher costs to the employer through an increased employer match. Some, in their focus on the current year's bottom line, can begin to see the expansion of the plan as a negative. However, when they step back to see the big picture and take into consideration the overall benefits to the company, a good plan becomes an overwhelming positive. For CFOs who serve on the fiduciary committee, as they often do, this is all the more reason to advocate for excellence on behalf of the participants. Though their focus on the committee must be solely in service to the plan's participants, they obviously also care about how the company fares. A good plan serves both interests.

"THIS IS HOW WE'VE ALWAYS DONE IT"

Despite those benefits that both employees and employers could gain through a 401(k) or 403(b) plan, not all plans are managed well. Many plans earn insufficient returns, cost more, and generally do not prepare employees well for retirement. Because of their weaknesses and vulnerabilities, those plans also are more likely to become a target for regulators and lawsuits. The opportunity cost is high, as no one is taking advantage of the potential benefits. Everyone misses out.

The troubling truth is that plan fiduciaries often lack the information they need to even know whether their plan is good. "This is the way we've always done it," they are told. And so the plan continues to operate the same as always—poorly.

That lack of quality and clarity is commonplace. Because the industry has not developed objective performance standards, serious problems can go unrecognized and unaddressed. As a result, investment lineups very often fail to perform as well as the indexes that reflect how well the markets in general are doing. In fact, in 2018, my company sponsored a study by the University of Missouri comparing the performance of 401(k) lineups to an all-index lineup, which is the benchmark that we recommend. The study initially focused on the years 2013 to 2015. In 2013, only 32 percent of plan investment lineups outperformed an all-index lineup; in 2014, only 12 percent did; and in 2015, 30 percent outperformed. In an update to the original study, we found that in 2016, 11 percent beat the benchmark, and in 2017, 83 percent did. We will update that study annually but suspect that the results likely will continue to be similar.[4]

Much has been written about the fact that actively managed

---

4 R. Yao, W. Wu, and C. Mendenhall, "Use of Advisors and Retirement Plan Performance," *Journal of Financial Counseling and Planning*, 31(1), 1-16. Table 4, Percentages of Plans that Outperformed Their Benchmark.

funds generally fail to outperform the indexes. That holds true for retirement plan lineups, but we don't hear much about that. When I got into this business, I observed that smaller plans approached investments with the sophistication of a typical individual—in other words, not a whole lot. As I worked my way up to $50 million plans, I presumed that I would find that the managers had been more savvy in their investment knowledge. They were not. Neither were the managers of the $500 million plans, when I got to that level.

Based upon what I have seen, fiduciary committee members typically are no more knowledgeable about investments than the population in general. If the committee has ten members, a few of them might have a greater level of sophistication, but most will have only a layman's understanding. Even among the few megaplans that separate the investment oversight into a separate committee, the level of understanding is generally akin to that of a hobbyist.

If you are like many committee members, when you hear that "we've always done it that way," you probably remain very quiet, presuming that people more knowledgeable than yourself already have ironed out the details. This book will get you out of the dark to reach the point where you can join the conversation confidently. You will know for certain whether the way it's being done is the way it should be done.

WHAT A GOOD PLAN LOOKS LIKE

How do you know whether the plan you oversee is, in fact, a good one? I wrote this book to answer that question. For now, understand that a good plan has three key elements.

THE PLAN'S INVESTMENT LINEUP PERFORMS WELL

A small gain in investment performance compounded over a plan participant's working career will have a tremendous impact on how much money will be available at retirement age. In chapter 6, we will see the dramatic influence that just half a percentage point change in the rate of return through the years can have on the balance. Compounding interest is powerful. It might seem mysterious, but it is a fact of mathematics.

THE TOTAL FEES PAID BY THE PLAN ARE LOW

The fees that participants must pay via the plan's expenses come right off the top of their earnings. Think of fees as a negative investment return. They sap the strength of the compounding effect. Just as a small gain in the percentage of return will boost retirement assets dramatically, a small drop in the percentage of return will reduce them dramatically. In chapter 7, we will take a close look at why fees matter so much and why they must be considered when assessing the quality of a retirement plan.

THE TOTAL CONTRIBUTIONS ARE AT AN APPROPRIATE LEVEL

As people scurry about their daily lives, they often neglect to think about how much they are setting aside for retirement. They fall victim to "short-termism," which has become a popular term for the phenomenon of focusing primarily on one's current needs and wants to the detriment of future concerns. No matter how stellar the performance of a plan, no matter how low the fees, no matter how generous the employer's match, nobody can successfully prepare for retirement without contributing regularly into their retirement account. Most people don't know how much they should be contributing. A good plan keeps track of how well its participants are contributing to the plan to be on pace to retire comfortably. Chapter 8 will explain how that works.

Those three elements work together in harmony in a good retirement plan. They must also be in proper balance. For example, a plan could spend hundreds of thousands of dollars for financial counseling services to help employees retire successfully, but such an expense would mean a significant rise in the fees that the plan must pay. The counseling would benefit the participants, but the higher fees would hurt them. In other words, don't get tunnel vision. There is a natural tension between the elements that make up a good plan, and you need to pay attention to all three of them. The positives must always prevail.

As a plan fiduciary, you are in a position to make sure that is happening. You oversee the management of the plan to ensure that it will allow workers to develop financial security so that they can retire on time. You must be aware and alert. Rest assured, you are up to the task. That is why you were selected for this role.

Above all, what qualifies you to serve is that you care about your colleagues who are pinning their retirement dreams on the success of the plan. That dedication to them needs to be in your heart. The rest you can learn.

THE BOTTOM LINE

- An employer-sponsored retirement plan is an important protection against financial insecurity. It can help people break the pattern of spending more than they earn.
- When employees are relieved of financial stress, they are better able to perform at their best levels, earn more, and advance in their careers. More productive employees also earn more money for their employers.
- A good retirement plan helps organizations attract and retain the best people.
- When older employees retire on time, organizations can bring in younger workers with fresh ideas at lower pay who are likely to stick around because they see advancement opportunities.
- Fiduciary committee members often lack the information to know whether their plan is a good one. Serious problems can go unaddressed because the industry lacks objective performance standards.
- A good plan has three key elements that must work in harmony: 1) The investment lineup performs well, 2) the total fees paid by the plan are low, and 3) the participants are contributing enough to be on pace to retire.

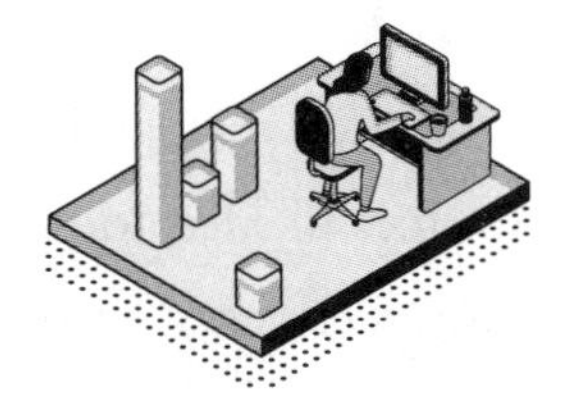

CHAPTER 2

THE ROOTS OF ERISA

Pension plans didn't exist in America when brothers Henry and Clement Studebaker opened a blacksmith shop in South Bend, Indiana. The first US private pension plan didn't come along until about twenty years later, in 1875. Fast forward a century, and pension plans had proliferated, and the Studebaker-Packard Corporation had become a national symbol of their "broken promise."

The company that evolved from supplying wagons to the army during the Civil War to become a well-known automaker was in trouble by the 1950s, struggling to compete with the Big Three dominating the market. In 1958, the company ended the retirement plan for employees of its Packard division and soon dropped the Packard marque from production. The workers were left with little or nothing in benefits, alerting the United Auto Workers (UAW) leadership of the need to protect the membership from default risk.

Five years later, it happened again when the company closed its last US assembly plant in South Bend, where it all started, and soon joined the ranks of DeSoto, Nash, and other automakers that had folded since World War II. After terminating seven thousand workers, the company terminated their retirement plans, too, but it had nowhere near the resources needed to pay the generous benefits that it had offered. Promises were easy. Funding them was another matter.

The Studebaker pension plan was so poorly funded, in fact, that about four thousand hourly workers received a lump sum of only 15 cents for every dollar that they had expected. That was despite having served the company, on average, nearly a quarter century. Three thousand workers with less than ten years on the job got nothing.

The presumption for millions of Americans working at major corporations with pension plans had long been that their jobs, and their retirement dreams, were secure. An increasing number, however, were coming to know better as some of those companies defaulted on their obligations. A demand for pension reform began to take root, though it was slow to grow.

In the Studebaker default of 1963, the UAW saw an opportunity to push for a legislative agenda to protect workers by insuring them against the risk of losing their pensions. At the time, no federal legislation regulated pension plans, and though a few states tried to do so, the result was a patchwork of inconsistent laws. Employee protection was next to nothing. If a company decided to end its retirement plan, or if the company was sold or went bankrupt, the workers might receive paltry benefits, if any, due to insufficient funding. Many companies required employees to work twenty or thirty years before they could get a pension, and any interruption in service, even a brief layoff or disability, could disqualify them. Some companies were known to dismiss workers just before they were vested to avoid paying the benefit.

The Studebaker case soon became a rallying cry for reform. Two years earlier, President John F. Kennedy already had set up a special investigative committee to begin studying the problems with pension plans, and now national attention was focusing on the issue. Then, in 1964, Teamsters boss Jimmy Hoffa was convicted of arranging large loans from the union's pension fund to leading organized crime figures. The publicity led to further reform and regulation initiatives in Washington, but it would be a decade before Congress took a decisive stance to protect workers.

That action came after increasing media attention, including an hour-long NBC report called *Pensions: The Broken Promise* that galvanized public sentiment. In the documentary, workers from around the country in a variety of industries told how they had been deprived of their benefits. The growing demand for reform became an outcry, and Congress initiated a series of public hearings. Within two years, it passed ERISA.

President Gerald R. Ford signed the act into law on Labor Day 1974. It was the country's first comprehensive corporate retirement plan legislation, establishing standards for private-sector pension plans. ERISA provisions required employers that offered pension plans to actually fund them and to vest the workers within ten years of service. In addition, the law required most private defined-benefit plans to insure against default through the Pension Benefit Guaranty Corporation (PBGC). If a company chooses to offer a retirement plan, the law said, it must operate it under fiduciary standards of conduct for the exclusive benefit of the participants and their beneficiaries.

ERISA has changed through the years with frequent amendments, but it remains the foundation of employee benefits law. The acronym often is used to refer broadly to the entire body of laws and regulations, many of them in the Internal Revenue Code, that deal with retirement benefits, as well as the precedents of case law and the policy changes made since the act's passage. Those provisions came too late to protect the workers at Studebaker and many other companies that abandoned their pension plans, but for countless others ERISA has championed just what its name proclaims: income security for their retirement.

THE DAWN OF THE 401(K) ERA

Just as no pension plans existed when the Studebaker brothers set up shop, there was no such thing as a 401(k) when ERISA became law. The pension plans that prevailed from the late 1800s through the 1970s generally paid workers a defined monthly benefit at retirement, funded by the employers. The ERISA provisions were written to address those traditional pension plans.

It's a new world. The original mission of that landmark legislation—to reform those defined-benefit pensions—has shifted to the regulation of the newer defined-contribution plans, in which the employees fund their own accounts. ERISA today covers both types of plans.

The fundamentals of how the defined-contribution plans operate is not all that complicated. The employee selects investments from a lineup of options and contributes to a personal account from his or her pay. Often, the employee gets a matching amount from the employer—most commonly, 50 cents on the dollar for contributions of up to 6 percent of pay. Initially, employee contributions were primarily made pretax, which means that the amount of the employee's contribution is not immediately subject to income tax, and the account continues to grow free of taxes. The taxes come after the employee retires and starts to withdraw the money. The presumption (sometimes a false one) is that he or she will be in a lower tax bracket then. Later, in 2001, with the passage of the Economic Growth and Tax Relief Reconciliation Act, plans could allow participants to choose to make some or all of the contributions into a Roth account. So-called Roth contributions are after-tax, meaning the employee pays the tax on the amount contributed, but then enjoys tax-free withdrawal later, under certain conditions.

Since arriving on the scene in the early 1980s, the 401(k) has become the predominant style of retirement plan. In the private sector, the traditional pension plan is becoming increasingly rare, although many public sector employees are covered by one. Though people tend to think of pensions as the old-style plans, the term describes both types—after all, the name of our company is Pension Consultants Inc. even though what we manage are primarily defined-contribution plans. Any retirement plan that is sponsored by an employer is a pension plan.

This revolution in retirement plans dates to the Revenue Act of 1978, which went into effect in 1980. Among its provisions, the act added an obscure subsection, 401(k), to the Internal Revenue Code that specified how employees could avoid taxation on income if they received it as deferred compensation, such as stock options, rather than direct pay.

Benefits consultant and attorney Ted Benna noticed the provision and saw an opportunity for employers to create tax-advantaged savings accounts for their workers. The tax code did not specifically allow that, however, so he petitioned the IRS for a modification allowing employees to set up tax-deferred accounts and contribute to them through salary deductions. The IRS agreed in 1981, and Benna set up the first 401(k) plan with his employer, the Johnson Companies. About fifty employees of the firm began making contributions that year from their paychecks.

Within a year, several large companies were offering employees the new 401(k) plans in which they could invest their deferred income without being taxed on the gains until withdrawing the money during retirement. The idea soon turned to a groundswell. Within two years, about half of all large firms were offering, or preparing to offer, a 401(k) plan. By 1990, the plans had 19 million participants with $384 billion in assets. Six years later, 30 million employees had a 401(k)-type plan, and assets topped $1 trillion.[5] In 2019, as the markets continued a historic decade-long bull run, assets in defined-contribution plans were well over $8 trillion.[6]

Many companies were eager to rid themselves of the old-style pension plans and get on the 401(k) bandwagon. They found the new plans to be less expensive for them and more predictable to fund. As retired employees and their spouses were living ever longer, employers were finding it increasingly costly to maintain a pool of capital to pay the pension benefits. The 401(k) gave companies an alternative that relieved them of responsibility for paying those retired workers.

Early in my career, throughout the 1990s, my colleagues and I dealt with a flood of companies that came to us seeking to either freeze or terminate their defined-benefit pension plans and start a 401(k). That was the decade when most companies switched over, although larger ones were doing so in the 1980s. From their perspec-

---

5 Kathleen Elkins, "A brief history of the 401(k), which changed how Americans retire," CNBC, January 4, 2017, https://www.cnbc.com/2017/01/04/a-brief-history-of-the-401k-which-changed-how-americans-retire.html.

6 Mark Nolan, "Retirement Assets Up First Quarter of 2019," My Solo 401k Financial, June 24, 2019, https://www.mysolo401k.net/retirement-assets-up-first-quarter-of-2019/.

tive, they were making enormous contributions every year into the pension funds, but they felt that the typical worker didn't seem to understand the value of what they were doing and didn't give them credit for it. They also found the variable annual cost to be difficult to predict and manage because of things beyond their control, such as market performance. Companies whose pension fund investments performed poorly and lost money had to make up the difference to keep the plan sufficiently funded. Those were the major reasons that executives were coming to us in those years to help them convert to a 401(k) plan for their workers. The proliferation of 401(k)-type plans transferred the investment risk to the workers, whether they were financially literate or not.

It's not that the defined-benefit pension plans were without risk, particularly in the pre-ERISA era, as the Studebaker debacle made readily apparent. Workers' retirement security depended upon whether the employer remained financially intact, and the pension plans were uninsured prior to the establishment of the federal PBGC, created under ERISA. Even if the company's fortunes were secure, the workers often were ineligible for benefits, and once eligible, they faced a long vesting schedule to build up to full benefits.[7] It's a common perception that in those days, workers tended to stay with the same employer for their whole career. That's just not true. The difference is that back then, people lost out on attractive pension benefits when they switched to a new job. They didn't stick around for the decade or so that it could take to lay claim to them. After ERISA, it typically took only about six years to become fully vested. Today, most of the plans that my company manages have either immediate vesting or a schedule of two or three years.

7 John W. Thompson, "Defined Benefit Plans at the Dawn of ERISA," Bureau of Labor Statistics, published March 30, 2005.

Those risks were what ERISA was designed to help remedy. Even today, though, many public employees—police officers, firefighters, teachers—face the prospect of losing their pension if their employer fails financially, as evidenced by high-profile cases of municipal bankruptcies. The funding ratios for state and municipal pension funds tend to be terrible, and public plans are not subject to ERISA. *The Wall Street Journal* reported in 2018 that state and city governments collectively had fallen an estimated $4 trillion short of what was promised to millions of public workers. That's about equal to the output of Germany's economy, the fourth largest in the world.[8] The risks of a defined-benefit pension plan were real then, and they are real today.

With the new plans, though, workers contended with a different type of risk. Besides the inherent market risk, they now found themselves as amateurs dabbling in the world of finance, which is risky by definition. They had to be capable of figuring out for themselves how much of their paychecks to contribute, long before they retired, to ensure that they would have enough money to see them through their old age. And they had to figure out how to invest that money. The company no longer took care of all that.

Besides the inherent market risk, they now found themselves as amateurs dabbling in the world of finance, which is risky by definition.

At first, many employees were suspicious of these new plans. Their reasoning was along these lines: "up till now I had a plan that the company paid for and it was free money for me, but now it

8 Sarah Krouse, "The Pension Hole for US Cities and States Is the Size of Germany's Economy," *The Wall Street Journal*, July 30, 2018, https://www.wsj.com/articles/the-pension-hole-for-u-s-cities-and-states-is-the-size-of-japans-economy-1532972501.

comes out of my paycheck, and it just doesn't seem fair." That attitude lingered until they started to see the tax advantages and the company matches coming into play as their accounts swelled. The initial resistance turned to widespread support.

A rip-roaring economy during many of those early years certainly helped to solidify that support. Strong market gains buoyed 401(k) accounts for years. From the late 1980s through the '90s, the stock market performance overall was strong, encouraging workers to get in on the action. All that new money pouring into the market from their paychecks strengthened the market further—in fact, the influx likely was a primary reason for the boom. The better the economy, the more money flowing in. The more money flowing in, the better the economy.

Then came the new millennium, when two recessions hit in the first decade. The slump in investments highlighted the fact that 401(k) savers were subject to the fluctuations of the markets and must make wise choices in their investments. Not everyone understood that. In their rush to divest themselves of their pension liability, companies tended to oversell the new product to their employees as a can't-lose proposition. This was a new industry that needed to mature and identify the issues it must address. That would take time.

By and large, the first generation of 401(k) account holders were left to their own devices as they made, or failed to make, key decisions about their futures. They sorely needed advice but didn't get much of it. Some did well regardless, grasping the tax deferral concept quickly and reaping the financial rewards. They accumulated far more than they ever would have received in monthly payments from a defined-benefit pension plan. Others learned the hard way that when it comes to the markets, losses go with the territory. New to this arena, they were far more vulnerable to error than the account holders in the generations that followed. Young people starting their careers today expect retirement planning to be hands-on. They have grown up in households where managing a 401(k) is talk around the table. They don't anticipate that the company will take care of them. Somebody who was mid-career in the early '80s had a much different perspective.

Nonetheless, in this era when defined-contribution plans have become the typical way Americans prepare for retirement, a widespread lack of financial literacy remains an issue. Millions of people who have little knowledge of investments must put their money to work wisely for their future, lest those savings evaporate. Many, however, make the wrong decisions for lack of savvy. Sometimes they just choose the first investment option they see on the lineup. Or they follow the lead of a coworker or friend, regardless of that person's age or circumstances. The result is that their savings fall short of their retirement needs.

Many people are not preparing for retirement at all or are failing to do so effectively. However, the Pension Protection Act of 2006 helped to change that situation by making it easier to enroll employees automatically. Some organizations, as an additional incentive to encourage participation, offer to automatically increase the rate of an employee's contributions by 1 percentage point a year, a barely noticeable boost that can add up to big bucks in the account over time. Those provisions have made a significant difference in participation rates in recent years.

THE EVOLUTION OF THE REGULATIONS

As the defined-contribution plans multiplied, so did federal regulations designed to deal with them. To all concerned, the 401(k) was a new phenomenon—to the employees, employers, and government regulators. All had to catch up with what was going on in the retirement planning arena.

Any major change can bring unintended consequences and the potential for abuse. A host of businesses evolved to service this new style of retirement plan, and a few of them were bad actors who soon discovered they could get a bigger piece of the action by withholding information or pitching it in a misleading way. As such situations transpired, the regulators issued new rules for how those service providers could operate in this new world. Congress passed new laws.

Today, many of those early abuses have been identified and curtailed, and further protections have been added for plan participants. This has been the natural evolution of a maturing industry. Some of the changes, in my estimation, have gone too far, but in balance the regulations have been for the better.

The evolution of the law continues as ERISA regulations and enforcement emphasize three fundamentals:

- **Participants must be provided with key information** about the plan, including its features and benefits. When that information is updated, the changes must be communicated to the participants.

- **Every plan must meet minimum standards** for features such as eligibility and vesting. The law defines how long a participant can be required to work for the employer before becoming eligible to participate in the plan, to begin accumulating benefits, and to gain a nonforfeitable right to those benefits.

- **Plan fiduciaries must meet standards of conduct.** ERISA defines the fiduciary as anyone who exercises control over the management of the plan or over its assets. Fiduciaries who violate those standards of conduct may be held personally liable.

In the decades since ERISA was created in 1974, a series of legislative initiatives have expanded its scope.

The Retirement Equity Act of 1984 authorized a spouse's rights to benefits, addressing concerns that plans had been treating women unfairly. Specifically, it established that retirement benefit plans are an asset for both the employee and the employee's spouse (or "alternative payee," such as an ex-spouse or dependent). In a divorce case, therefore, the money that a participant has in a plan must be taken into consideration during the distribution of assets. The act also addressed concerns that many women were not getting vested because they had left their jobs to raise their kids, and that widows were being denied benefits when their spouses died before retiring. New rules lowered the minimum age requirement for plan participation, increased the years of service counted for vesting purposes, prevented plans from counting parental leave as a break in service for participation and vesting, and made survivor benefits automatic unless the spouse waived that right.

In 2001, the Economic Growth and Tax Relief Reconciliation Act, which the George W. Bush administration designed to stimulate the economy with tax cuts, resulted in several more significant changes to the 401(k). The law allowed individuals and companies to contribute more to the account, and it also allowed participants age fifty or older to make catch-up contributions. The amounts have been adjusted annually for inflation. For 2020, the general annual employee contribution limit is $19,500, plus $6,500 for catch-up.

The Pension Protection Act (PPA) of 2006 instituted the most significant reforms to pension plans since the establishment of ERISA thirty-two years earlier. Generally, the PPA provisions aimed to further protect retirement accounts and strengthen the pension system overall. The act established rules for investment advice to participants, expanded requirements for disclosures to participants, and created a default investment procedure when participants do not make selections from the lineup. In addition, the PPA began holding companies more accountable for underfunding their existing defined-benefit plans. To save money, some companies had been taking advantage of loopholes in the law to cut funding for the pension plans and skip payments to the PGBC. The act requires organizations that are guilty of underfunding to pay higher premiums for the PGBC insurance.

The PPA's establishment of the automatic contribution arrangements has had a major impact on public policy by getting workers to take the reins of their own retirement. The act formalized and gave legal blessing to the negative election that some plans already had instituted, in which new employees would join the plan and have a certain percentage of their pay withheld unless they specifically elected not to participate. The provision got many more people saving for retirement who otherwise might not have set aside a cent, and it encouraged employers to focus more on educating this influx of new participants on their investment options. More on the auto-enroll features in chapter 8.

DEALING WITH THE REGULATORS AND ENFORCERS

The two primary federal agencies given authority over regulating and enforcing ERISA are the IRS and the Department of Labor (DOL), which coordinate their activities. The IRS primarily looks at participation, vesting, and funding issues, and it reviews retirement plan documents to assure plan sponsors that they are written by the rules. The DOL primarily enforces the fiduciary rules governing the conduct of plan managers and investigates prohibited transactions. Meanwhile, the PBGC insures a guaranteed minimum benefit for certain defined-benefit pension plans.

The DOL can audit plans for fiduciary compliance. It can levy fines if it discovers a significant breach where an action or inaction has hurt plan participants. The IRS also can audit plans but focuses more on matters that relate to the tax treatment of plans. Both agencies can pass regulations formally but also issue a series of guidances that reflect their interpretations of the law, each year averaging a dozen or two in all. They come at a frequent pace, and it is essential that the plan sponsors and fiduciary committees pay attention to them so that they remain in compliance.

Those guidances can be vague and difficult to interpret, yet they are meant to clarify specific actions that plan sponsors and fiduciary committees should be taking. On the fiduciary committee, your job is to hire competent counsel and a good recordkeeper to keep up with those expectations. Your responsibility is to regularly check in with those professionals, even though you won't know every jot or tittle yourself. Good managers delegate. They do not try to personally attend to every detail of what must be done within the organization. Likewise, you are fulfilling your duty if you persist in asking your experts whether there is anything outstanding that must be addressed due to the new guidances that come streaming in.

The death sentence for a retirement plan is for the government to rule it disqualified. That is an exceedingly rare happening, because the authorities realize the difficult consequences of such a severe action for so many people involved in the plan. If, for example, the IRS determines that an organization's 401(k) is so poorly compliant with the rules of ERISA that it must be disqualified, all the contributions that participants made into their accounts through the years no longer qualify for tax-advantaged treatment. In fact, every employee would have to amend his or her previous tax filings to reflect the fact that the contributions for those years no longer were deductible—and the employer match was now taxable income. This would be true for every year the plan is deemed disqualified. In a word, it's a mess, and it only happens in cases of egregious noncompliance.

Short of that, the enforcers can take a whole spectrum of actions. Both the IRS and DOL have programs where organizations can self-report. If an organization becomes aware of a problem with its retirement plan, it can 'fess up and clean up—and the agencies provide instructions on how to set things straight. It's another matter if the agencies find the problem themselves during an audit. They will institute the cleanup procedure, and they are more likely to issue fines and penalties, which could be for both civil and criminal violations.

Other than disqualification, most of the regulatory infractions will be relatively minor, and the resolution will amount to the organization's doing for the plan what it should have done anyway. For example, if a company has been enrolling new employees after a year rather than after three months as required by the plan, it will have to abide by a formula to make that up to them. That can be a significant amount of money, but that is only what it would have cost had things been done right all along. The additional fines and penalties in such cases tend to be relatively minimal. Every year, our company does have clients who get audited by the Department of Labor, but never have we seen a member of a fiduciary committee held liable for breach of responsibility.

A bigger concern, as we will see in chapter 4, has been lawsuits filed by plan participants. These have become more prevalent in the last decade, and they are coming down the pike at a faster pace. The plaintiffs and their attorneys have been targeting poorly run plans across the nation. That's the real threat, outside the realm of the regulators, that could drain away big dollars from organizations that have failed to follow the rules. There is a remedy, of course. Provide a good plan. If you and your colleagues on the fiduciary committee meet regularly, keep an agenda of matters to review, and ask plenty of pertinent questions about investments and fees and procedures, you are providing responsible oversight. Do it right, and you need not fear legal repercussions.

As for the flow of new regulations, many of them will apply only to a small number of plans, and unless yours is one of them, your committee probably will not be presented with the information. If a regulation directly impacts your particular retirement plan, the attorney, recordkeeper, and plan adviser should be aware of it and notify you of the change, which often amounts to just adding some language to update the plan document. As a fiduciary committee member, you will not be inundated with such minor changes and may not be aware of them. At your next meeting, your committee should be informed of anything that pertains to your organization's plan and that requires your fiduciary oversight. If you have a good team in place, you will be fine.

We have come a long way since the days when workers labored

for years under the illusion that they would be set for life thanks to their company's pension plan. In the early days, a promise was not always what it seemed, and though many workers did retire comfortably, many others felt the sting of disappointment as their retirement dreams came to naught. Today, with protections of federal law in place for nearly half a century and continual refinements expanding ERISA's reach and plugging up loopholes, employees can plan for the future with far greater confidence. That is true with the old-style pension plans that pay retirees a defined benefit monthly, and it is equally true in this day of 401(k) and related plans where workers save and invest their own way to retirement success. ERISA, for all its complexity and perplexity, has helped countless people get a better night's sleep.

THE BOTTOM LINE

- The Studebaker pension plan default of 1963 focused attention on pension plan abuses and led to calls for reform.
- The Employee Retirement Income Security Act of 1974, or ERISA, established standards for private-sector pension plans, including the fiduciary obligation to operate them for the exclusive benefit of participants and their beneficiaries.
- Frequently amended through the years, ERISA remains the foundation of employee benefit law.
- The Revenue Act of 1978 ushered in the era of the 401(k)-style defined-contribution plans that have replaced many of the old-style defined-benefit pension plans. Many companies were eager to make the transition.
- The defined-contribution plans shifted the burden of retirement planning and investing from the employers to the employees, many of whom lack financial sophistication.
- The Department of Labor and the Internal Revenue Service are the two primary federal agencies given authority to regulate and enforce the provisions of ERISA.
- The laws and regulations that have sought to stem abuses help employees today plan for retirement with far greater confidence than in previous generations.

CHAPTER 3

THE RULES OF THE GAME

The Massachusetts Institute of Technology wasn't playing by the rules, according to a group of employees with money invested in its retirement plan, and the university, rather than proceed to trial, agreed to pay $18.1 million in damages.

The MIT case, which worked its way through the courts for three years before the settlement in late 2019, was like many other lawsuits claiming that plan fiduciaries made decisions that hurt participants financially. This one, however, added a new twist: the class action alleged what amounted to a kickback scheme—a *quid pro quo* between the university and Fidelity Investments.

During the time that it was recordkeeper for the 403(b) plan, Fidelity donated more than $23 million to MIT's endowment—but those donations were buying favorable treatment, the employees claimed. In exchange, they said, MIT ensured that Fidelity could charge excessive fees that cost the plan participants millions of dollars.

The lawsuit said Fidelity became the recordkeeper without competitive bidding. It pointed out that Abigail Johnson, the chief executive officer and co-owner of Fidelity, was a lifetime member of the university's board of trustees. At one point, according to a court filing, MIT was considering a consultant's advice to remove a Fidelity fund from the lineup. Fidelity representatives took the chairperson of MIT's fiduciary committee to a Boston Celtics game, the filing said, where they emphasized their partnership while keeping Ms. Johnson apprised of the outing and the discussion.

Shortly before the trial was to begin, MIT decided that a settlement would be the smartest way to go, although it still maintained that it had met all its fiduciary requirements under ERISA.

Nonetheless, as part of the deal the university agreed to provide regular training every year for the plan fiduciaries so that they understood ERISA, its regulations, and their obligations to make decisions exclusively in the best interests of plan participants. MIT agreed to get a new recordkeeper and to prohibit that firm from approaching the participants to talk about other products and services.

The MIT employees were represented by Schlichter Bogard & Denton LLP, a law firm based in St. Louis, Missouri, that initiated a wave of litigation against major universities challenging their management of retirement plans. Among them, Vanderbilt University settled for $14.5 million, Johns Hopkins for $14 million, and Duke for $10.65 million.[9]

9 Nevin Adams, "Schlichter Wrangles Biggest 403(b) Excessive Fee Settlement Yet," NAPA, October 30, 2019, https://www.napa-net.org/news-info/daily-news/schlichter-wrangles-biggest-403b-excessive-fee-settlement-yet; Jacklyn Wille, "MIT Inks Largest Settlement in College Retirement Plan Lawsuits," Bloomberg Law, October 29, 2019, https://news.bloomberglaw.com/employee-benefits/mit-inks-largest-settlement-in-college-retirement-plan-lawsuits; "MIT Squanders Workers' Retirement Savings in Payments to Abigail Johnson and Fidelity in

The case highlights the importance of maintaining fiduciary responsibility and complying with the big-picture standards established in ERISA. In summary, they are: managing the plan solely in the interests of the participants and their beneficiaries, managing the plan prudently, diversifying the investments to reduce the risk of large losses, and abiding by the governing documents of the plan so long as they are consistent with ERISA law. These standards are mostly broad in order to give guidance to fiduciaries about proper intent. Their application can only be assessed on a case-by-case basis.

However, the last standard listed, abiding by the governing documents of the plan, isn't broadly defined. It is very specific. In this chapter, we will look at those governing documents and how a well-functioning plan operates under them.

SO WHO RUNS THE SHOW?

As you get started in your role as a plan fiduciary, you need to know that there are limitations to your power. From the very inception of your organization's plan, certain rules were already set in place. Those rules primarily involve the choices of the employer who sponsors the plan and the fiduciaries like you who are responsible for managing it. In short, the employer creates the plan and chooses its provisions. The fiduciaries administer the plan. Neither, however, has unchecked authority. Once a plan is set up, they must follow its provisions, as well as the numerous laws and regulations governing retirement plans.

The legal term for the plan sponsor is settlor, meaning the one who settles, or establishes, the plan—and in most cases, that is the employer. The term is used in reference to trusts, and a 401(k) plan is

---

Return for Donations, Says Schlichter Bogard & Denton," Businesswire, August 5, 2019, https://www.businesswire.com/news/home/20190805005670/en/MIT-Squanders-Workers%E2%80%99-Retirement-Savings-Payments-Abigail.

a trust, since the participants' money is being held and managed by another party on their behalf.

Essentially, the settlor makes the rules governing the plan. These rules are often called the terms and conditions of the plan. Once the terms and conditions are established, the fiduciaries (you and your fellow committee members) are charged with operating the plan. In doing so, you must always see that it doesn't deviate from those terms and conditions.

As a result of this legal governance structure, the settlor can make decisions about the plan that will impact the organization from a business perspective. You, the fiduciary, cannot. You must make your decisions solely in the interest of the plan's participants and beneficiaries and must not consider what might be best for the organization.

For example, let's say your employer, hoping for favorable terms on a loan, proposes to your committee that its banker be selected as recordkeeper or investment provider for the plan. As a fiduciary, your responsibility is to speak up and say no—not just sit back in silence figuring that a bank is a bank and you want to keep your job. It's your duty to point out the inherent conflict of interest. In the real world, though, fiduciary committee members may just go along with whatever the CEO or CFO wants to do. In practice, they often choose service providers not on their merits but on what they can provide to the employer. That should never happen. Self-dealing can lead to loads of trouble, as we have seen and will see again in the next chapter.

Here are some examples of legitimate decisions that the settlor makes:

- **Offering a retirement plan in the first place.** As obvious as that might seem, a lot of people do not realize that their employer is under no obligation to provide them with a retirement plan.

Employers offer such plans as part of their benefits package so that they can remain competitive in attracting talent and because they truly wish to help their people prepare for a fruitful retirement. It is a valuable benefit, but it is not an entitlement.

- **Choosing the terms and conditions of the plan.** For example, the employer will decide when employees become eligible to participate and their vesting schedule. The employer will decide whether to match their contributions and at what percentage. Such choices influence the cost to the organization for providing the benefit.
- **Voluntarily amending the terms and conditions.** The employer may decide to raise or lower the percentage of the match and on how much of an employee's deferred compensation it can be applied. Let's say the plan document originally established that the company would add a 50 percent match to contributions of up to 6 percent of the deferred compensation. If the company decides to apply the match on up to 8 percent of deferred compensation, it can choose to change that provision. Perhaps the company decides to make employees eligible for the plan immediately upon their hiring rather than waiting a year. Those are examples of voluntary amendments to the terms and conditions.
- **Terminating the plan.** This happens, though not often. It's more common in recessionary periods when organizations face financial distress and file for bankruptcy. Employees may fear they will lose their money, but it has been held in trust and will be distributed to them as it would if they were leaving the company or retiring. Just because the company is going under doesn't mean the assets in the plan will vanish.

The fiduciary committee can pay for expenses associated with managing the plan by charging them against plan assets. In doing so, however, it has a duty to look out for the participants' best interests. However, the employer must not charge expenses against the plan assets. The company may face costs, for example, from voluntarily amending the plan, but it must pay for those on its own tab. An occasional exception would be a major change in ERISA law that requires a rewrite of the plan documents. Because such an expense is not a voluntary one, it could be charged to the plan.

THE RETIREMENT PLAN RULEBOOK

The settlor's rules are written in a comprehensive legal document. It can be called different things depending on who drafted it for the settlor. For our purposes here, we will call it the plan document. Along with the terms and conditions, it contains numerous definitions and procedures.

Most organizations use a format that the Internal Revenue Service has preapproved for compliance. Typically, the preapproved plan includes a basic plan and trust document, along with another document that details the various choices that employers can make for provisions they wish to include, such as the match rate and rules for eligibility and enrollment. Those choices collectively are often called the adoption agreement. That package becomes the legal foundation for a retirement plan.

Most employers are served well with one of the variations of a preapproved plan. Those few that have a unique requirement—for example, they wish to establish different percentage contributions for their highly paid employees—can have an attorney draft a customized plan document that they may subsequently submit for approval.

The plan document is central to the operation of your retirement plan, and you need to be familiar with its provisions. To do a good job, you need to learn the rules and understand the basic terms and conditions of your plan so that your decisions and management will be consistent with them.

Educate yourself, but know your limitations. Even if it seems impractical for your committee to become expert on every provision listed in the plan document, you do need to be expert at recognizing when to consult a lawyer. For help with matters that you are not able to address, you should hire an attorney who specializes and is experienced in ERISA law.

When in doubt, always seek legal counsel. Questions frequently arise about how to apply a term or condition to the situation at hand. For example, what happens when an employee terminates and is due a severance payment? Should you withhold from that severance payment and match the contribution? What about payment for unused vacation days? Your organization's benefits staff will carry out those provisions, but your committee still has the fiduciary responsibility of oversight. In other words, you must make sure the job gets done correctly, including any unusual requirements. Since you probably are not an expert on such matters, it's time to contact the lawyer. For more information on hiring an ERISA specialist, see chapter 5.

Altogether, the plan document, along with the associated agreements, will be a couple of hundred pages long, and it is not written for your reading pleasure. It is dense material, packed with legalese, that provides comprehensive instructions for whatever might come up in the administration of the plan. The language is precise but can be difficult to decipher for anyone without a juris doctorate. In recognition of that concern, ERISA requires that all plans include another document, known as the Summary Plan Description.

THE SUMMARY PLAN DESCRIPTION

The Summary Plan Description, or SPD, is a relatively brief overview of the retirement plan's benefits and how it works. The SPD lists the relevant provisions that you will face day to day. Typically ten to twenty pages, it is not as comprehensive as the plan document and must be written in plain, understandable language.

Though the SPD does not cover every detail of the plan's terms and conditions, it will give you the foundation that you need, and it will help you to recognize important issues on which you require further legal guidance. If serving on a fiduciary committee is a new experience for you, the document will help you get up to speed quickly so that you can participate confidently and meaningfully in discussions. The SPD is not a substitute for the official plan document. It is a supplement that hits the highlights. From there, you and your legal counsel can delve into the details as necessary.

The intent of the SPD requirement is to cut through any confusion, and not just for the fiduciaries. The participants and beneficiaries often will have questions about how the plan works and about their benefits, responsibilities, and rights. By making sure that they can get their answers easily and clearly, the SPD reduces the number of calls that the human resources staff must field. Greater clarity forestalls complaints and lawsuits.

The SPD therefore is the main vehicle for communicating with participants and beneficiaries about a retirement plan. To ensure that they are fully informed, ERISA has established rules for distributing copies to them. New participants in an existing plan must receive a copy of the SPD within ninety days of becoming covered by the plan. A new beneficiary must receive a copy within ninety days of commencing benefits. At any time that a participant or beneficiary requests a copy, it must be provided within thirty days. If the employer is establishing a new plan, the SPD must be provided to the participants within 120 days of the official startup. Additional distribution is required every five or ten years, depending on whether changes have been made to the SPD or not.

Since it is relatively short and easy to read, you should review the SPD from time to time to become familiar with your plan's terms and conditions. You should also take a copy with you to all committee meetings and refer to it often.

The Department of Labor requires that the SPD include a variety of information, such as whether the company provides matching contributions, at what percentages, and under what conditions; when employees become eligible to participate and the vesting schedule; how to claim benefits and how they are calculated and paid; and employees' legal rights, including guidance on filing a grievance or an appeal.

POLICY DOCUMENTS

Two additional documents often included in a retirement plan are an investment policy statement and a loan policy.

ERISA does not require plans to have written investment policy statements, but they are common in the industry. At Pension Consultants, we have all of our clients sign one. It describes the general characteristics that we seek when we are selecting investments for the plan and sets forth how we will monitor them. It lists the asset classes that we will offer and the benchmarks for assessing our performance in each of them. Our investment policy statement is typically six or seven pages. The regulations, however, do not specify what a plan sponsor or fiduciary committee must include in the statement if it chooses to have one at all.

Some retirement plans allow the participants to borrow money against the assets in their accounts. If your plan offers them such loans, you must have a policy that governs the details. The loan policy sometimes is written as part of the plan documents and sometimes is drafted separately. It should spell out the interest calculation and the terms and expectations for repayment of a loan to the account.

WATCH OUT FOR CHANGES

Now and then, an organization runs into a troubling situation in which it discovers that it has failed to abide by a rule for its retirement plan, sometimes for years, and must go back to make amends. For example, the company match has been applied at a lower rate than specified, shortchanging the participants who lost out not only on the additional contribution but on the potential investment return that they might have received. Or sometimes the wrong definition of employee compensation has been used in calculating the percentages for a match. Such situations happen often enough that the regulators have prescribed how to clean up the problem without running afoul of the law.

Not following the rules of the plan document is a common issue, and it often happens when the organization decides to make changes but fails to properly amend the plan document.

Not following the rules of the plan document is a common issue, and it often happens when the organization decides to make changes but fails to properly amend the plan document. Sometimes the document has been amended properly but the benefits department, unaware that the terms have changed, continues to administer the provisions the same way. That can happen either because of a lapse in communication or because of turnover in the staff.

As a plan fiduciary, you must be alert to the potential that the terms and conditions of your plan will change occasionally. There are three primary causes for changes to the plan's documents:

- **Updates in laws or regulations.** Whenever a new law or regulation impacts employer retirement plans, the language in the plan's documents may need to be amended. These changes can be minimal or may require an entire rewrite, which is called a restatement. The IRS tends to require restatements of the entire plan document every ten to fifteen years as the smaller changes accumulate. The responsibility for ensuring that the retirement plan complies with those changes usually falls on the fiduciary committee. The fiduciary committee generally learns about changes to the plan from the benefits staff and the human resources director, who will be the contact people getting the notifications. The importance of good communication is one more reason that the committee should meet regularly.
- **A new attorney or other service provider.** If the employer hires a new attorney or if your committee hires a new recordkeeper, the incoming firm may want to use its own set of plan documents. If you were to keep your existing documents, the new provider likely would charge a lot more to deal with wording and provisions with which it was not familiar. To avoid that, your organization likely would make the switch. As a fiduciary, you must check that all the provisions in the old document make their way into the new one. In practice, changes often get through unnoticed, such as the definition of compensation.

- **An amendment by the employer.** The settlor may revise the plan to establish a new rule or to change an existing one. For example, the organization decides to change how much deferred compensation it will match, or how soon new employees will be eligible to begin contributing to the plan. Any such changes to the terms and conditions must be amended in the documents.

Again, be extremely careful whenever changes have been made to your plan's documents. It is your job to ensure that the plan operates as prescribed. If you miss something, the consequences can be costly. Let's say a retirement plan begins operating under a new set of documents, but the fiduciary committee fails to notice until two years later that new employees have become eligible to sign up after three months of service instead of six months—and the benefits staff has been enforcing the old provision. To correct that error, the company must presume that the new hires would have joined sooner and must pay them for the missed deferral opportunity and any additional match that they would have received as well as an estimation of their lost investment earnings. The amount would be based on a formula calculating the average contribution. A large employer with high turnover could easily be required to put millions of dollars into the plan—and it will cost more if the error turns up in an audit. The remedy is easier to swallow when an organization discovers the error itself and complies voluntarily.

With so many retirement plans operating across the country, it's safe to say that such predicaments are surfacing every day. Prevention is the best medicine. To fulfill your watchdog role, you must be aware of what is going on, and that requires good communication all around. When you hear that a term has been changed, check your copy of the SPD and make sure the document reflects the amendment. If you do not see the change, ask for a revised copy. At the committee meeting, ask whoever is responsible for the daily administration of the plan whether the change has been made in the plan documents. If the answer is yes, that response should be officially recorded in the minutes of the meeting.

You also will need to confirm that the change intended was the only change made. Sometimes the person or firm that drafts the documents on behalf of the settlor will unintentionally change other aspects of the terms and conditions. Years can go by before it is discovered that the plan has been operating outside the rules established in the documents. To prevent such a headache, scrutinize any document changes to make sure that they have not inadvertently altered other provisions.

In such situations, your ERISA attorney is invaluable. He or she will review the documents and attest to whether the terms and conditions are up to date, consistent, and in good standing. And if you include the lawyer's perspective in the minutes of your committee meeting, you will be making strides toward establishing that you have been playing by the rules.

THE BOTTOM LINE

- The employer establishes the retirement plan and its rules—its terms and conditions. The fiduciary committee operates it. Once the plan is set up, both must strictly abide by those rules and the many laws and regulations that govern retirement plans.
- The employer can make decisions about the plan from a business perspective. The fiduciaries, however, must make all their decisions solely in the best interest of the participants and beneficiaries.
- The fiduciaries can use assets of the plan to pay for the various costs of managing it, so long as they do so in the participants' best interest. The employer, however, generally cannot use plan assets to pay for expenses involved in amending the plan.
- The plan document is the long and comprehensive legal rulebook for the plan, explicitly stating the terms and conditions in dense and precise legal language.
- The Summary Plan Description is a relatively brief overview of the plan. It is written in plain, understandable language and is the primary means of communicating the plan's benefits and provisions to the participants and beneficiaries.
- Failure to follow the rules is a common issue and often happens when the employer changes a provision but doesn't properly amend the plan document. It also can happen if the benefits staff is unaware of a change in rules. The fiduciary committee must be alert to any such updates.

CHAPTER 4

KEEPING OUT OF TROUBLE

For the first quarter century of defined-contribution plans, lawsuits against their sponsors and fiduciaries were rare. Then, in 2006, along came eight. The next year, eighteen—and one hundred seven more in 2008.[10] Clearly, somebody had figured out how to push for fiduciary accountability, particularly from defendants with deep pockets.

That somebody was Schlichter Bogard & Denton, the Missouri law firm that later would file the case against MIT we discussed in chapter 3. The Schlichter firm has made ERISA litigation its signature work since establishing that plan participants have the legal standing to sue. The firm initiated that first wave in 2006 and filed many of

10 Russ Wiles, "Here's why so many workers are suing employers over 401(k) plans," AZ Central, August 25, 2019, https://www.azcentral.com/story/money/business/consumers/2019/08/25/401-k-plan-lawsuits-rise-unhappy-employees-retirement-investment-options/2064025001/.

the ensuing suits, leading the way for copycat lawyers to join the fray. Many of the early cases—nearly all of those filed in 2008, for example—alleged inappropriate investments. As the economy slid to recessionary depths, the litigants naturally focused on the performance of securities that were made available to the plan's participants.

However, some of the cases in that first round of class actions took a tack that no US law firm ever had tried against a 401(k). Nor had the Department of Labor made such a claim. The first to do so was *Tussy v. ABB*. The plaintiffs complained not only that the investments were inappropriate but also that the fiduciaries had allowed excessive fees. In the years since, that allegation has become the most prevalent grounds for hundreds of lawsuits filed against 401(k)-type retirement plans, and the tide is still coming in.

This chapter is not about controlling fees, however, nor is it about offering appropriate investments. We will examine both of those later. This chapter is about avoiding the legal trouble that has dogged more and more retirement plans. We will discuss some of the legal requirements that you face in your role as a plan fiduciary. *Tussy v. ABB* demonstrates how questionable management of fees can land a plan fiduciary in the courtroom, but that's just one way to get there. As we look at the ABB case, remember this overarching lesson: the way to keep a retirement plan out of trouble is simply knowing how to do a good job—and doing it. Nothing need be questionable.

The complex case against ABB Group, a multinational corporation in the field of robotics technology and heavy electrical equipment, wound its way through the federal courts for thirteen years. It was the first and one of the only 401(k) cases to go to trial, and the plaintiffs won a $36.9 million judgment in 2012. After years of appeals, the parties agreed in 2019 on a $55 million settlement, among the largest in litigation over fees. In 2015, Boeing Co. settled for $57 million and

Lockheed Martin Corp. for $62 million.

In essence, the ABB lawsuit accused the company of using the savings of its employees and retirees to subsidize its own corporate expenses. The plaintiffs sued the plan fiduciaries and recordkeeper, as well as Fidelity Investments and the Fidelity investment adviser.

According to the lawsuit, the fiduciaries decided to replace the Vanguard Wellington Fund with the Fidelity Freedom Funds—a series of target date funds. They then mapped, or moved, $123 million, nearly a tenth of the total plan assets, from the former to the latter, although participants could choose a different option at any time. The court ruled that the decision was based on the company's self-interest and therefore a breach of fiduciary duty.

Specifically, the court found that the fiduciaries had agreed to let the 401(k) participants overpay for Fidelity's services as the plan's recordkeeper. In return for getting a sweet spot on the investment menu, the court said, Fidelity gave ABB a break on pricing for services that the company bought for itself, such as recordkeeping for a corporate pension plan and payroll processing.

The court found that the fiduciaries had not properly monitored and controlled those recordkeeping expenses. It ordered an extensive reform of the 401(k) to reduce the fees. In addition, the court required ABB to seek competitive bids to hire a new recordkeeper for the plan who would not provide the company with any corporate services. In selecting investments, the court ordered, the fiduciaries must choose the share class with the lowest expense ratio.

ABB got in trouble, in part, by failing to follow its own rules. In its investment policy statement, the company had declared that it would provide the participants with a menu of the lowest-cost available funds. Its failure to do so led to its failure to prevail in court—and to a $55 million blow to the company's bottom line. It was a tough lesson, but all in all the case is among those that have influenced the retirement plan industry to make changes for the better as it presses for reduced costs and greater transparency.

GOOD LAWYER, GOOD INSURANCE

If you haven't already done so, your committee should hire an attorney who has experience working with qualified retirement plans and especially one who is familiar with the ins and outs of ERISA. You and your fellow committee members should not be playing amateur lawyer. The laws and regulations are complex and require knowledgeable legal advice. In a few extreme cases, noncompliance has resulted in a plan becoming disqualified, which can have severe tax ramifications for the participants.

The laws and regulations are complex and require knowledgeable legal advice.

Almost all the ERISA attorneys who assist fiduciary committees were originally engaged by the plan sponsor, either to draft the plan document or review it. In other words, the lawyer's client is the employer—and although that is the norm, it is not what I recommend. ERISA anticipates that the fiduciary committee will operate independently from the plan sponsor. My recommendation is that the fiduciary committees should hire their own lawyer to be present at committee meetings, and they can spend plan assets to do so. As I see it, that prevents divided loyalties. It forestalls the potential for conflict between the employer's interests and the best interests of the plan participants.

When litigants take a retirement plan to court, the tactic tends to be to sue everybody at first. They will likely sue the plan sponsor, the organization's officers, the fiduciary committee as a whole, and the individual committee members. For that reason, in addition to working with an experienced ERISA attorney, your committee should obtain fiduciary liability insurance, which covers you personally against claims that you have breached your duties. The employer often pays the premium, but it also can be paid by an employee organization or from plan assets. It should be noted, however, that paying the insurance premium from plan assets is fraught with legal peril. Don't try it unless under the close supervision of legal counsel. An individual fiduciary also can buy a personal policy.

Although fiduciary liability insurance is not an ERISA requirement, I would not serve on a committee without it unless the employer had indemnified me in writing. ERISA allows employers to do that for fiduciaries so long as they do not claim to be relieving them of responsibility and liability. The employer can only agree to pay for that liability if it is incurred. That arrangement has the same effect as insurance.

Note that fiduciary insurance is not the same as an ERISA fidelity bond, which all plans must obtain for protection from loss due to fraud or dishonesty. Imagine a scenario where a benefits employee is in charge of preparing documents for distribution of assets to Fred, a plan participant who has left the company. Cindy falsifies the documents to instruct the plan custodian to send those assets to an account under her control at a local bank. The custodian complies, and Cindy withdraws the money—and then she's gone. Here's another scenario: An employer that is having financial trouble withholds money from paychecks but never sends it into the plan. Desperately trying to stay afloat, the employer may hope to make it up later—but it's still fraud, and it happens. That's why plans with more than a hundred participants are required to get an annual audit.

And that's why ERISA requires a fidelity bond. The bond should be the lesser of 10 percent of assets or $500,000.

STANDARDS OF FIDUCIARY CONDUCT

In chapter 3, we discussed the role of the employer in establishing a plan and preparing the documents that set forth the terms and conditions, as well as your role as a plan fiduciary in implementing those rules and protecting the interests of the participants.

ERISA stipulates specific standards by which you must act. It says:

- You must run the plan solely in the interest of participants and beneficiaries and for the exclusive purpose of providing benefits and paying plan expenses.
- You must act prudently and must diversify the plan's investments in order to minimize the risk of large losses.
- At all times, you must abide by the governing documents of the plan so long as they are consistent with ERISA law.
- You must avoid conflicts of interest.[11]

The words *exclusive purpose* are critical here. Nothing should motivate and guide your decisions other than the interests of the plan participants. You must not hire service providers because they are your friends or because anyone has promised some benefit to you or your employer. Doing so is begging for trouble. Mostly such transgressions happen because committee members don't know any better, but ignorance of your ERISA duties is no excuse.

Managing the plan's costs is also an important function. Whether those are expenses charged by service providers or related to the invest-

11 "Fiduciary Responsibilities," US Department of Labor, accessed April 23, 2020, www.dol.gov/general/topic/retirement/fiduciaryresp.

ments, they must be kept reasonably low. In chapters 6 and 7, we will take a close look at how you can make sure that you are fulfilling that responsibility.

ERISA requires you to manage the plan with "care, skill, prudence, and diligence." A good way to demonstrate that is to document how and why you are making plan management decisions. Those decisions won't always be the best in hindsight. When selecting investments, for example, that's the way it often goes—but never rush your decisions. A prudent and well-documented process is the best way to defend yourself if someone claims you have been careless. Show that your committee has been reasonable and thorough in asking questions, seeking advice, and talking it through. Be sure that your committee is keeping minutes of every meeting.

THE RISK OF CIVIL OR CRIMINAL ACTION

Failure to meet the ERISA standards could result in either civil or criminal action against the plan fiduciaries that could result in fines and penalties, including prison. The Department of Labor is in large part responsible for the enforcement of the various provisions of the law.

Here are some examples of violations that might prompt a DOL civil action:

- **Failure to operate the plan for the exclusive benefit of the participants.** You must not self-deal. You cannot benefit personally from any of your decisions or actions, and you cannot use plan assets to benefit parties related to the plan, such as the plan sponsor or any of your fellow fiduciaries.
- **Failure to properly value the plan's assets or to hold them in trust.** The assets must be valued at least annually. Mutual

funds, of course, are valued daily, but some plans, particularly at very small companies, hold assets such as property.

- **Failure to properly select and monitor the activities of the plan's service providers.** You have an ongoing duty to track expenses. A provider that charged a reasonable amount twenty years ago might not be offering such a good deal now that the plan has grown from $5 million in assets to $250 million.
- **Taking an adverse or punitive action against a participant for exercising his/her rights under the plan.** Participants must not be fired, be demoted, be denied a bonus or pay, or receive any other penalty for availing themselves of their rights as spelled out by ERISA and the plan documents.

Here are some examples of violations that might prompt the DOL to file a criminal enforcement:

- **Stealing or embezzling** plan assets.
- **Making false statements or concealing facts** from an enforcement agency. Liars do not fare well when caught.
- **Taking kickbacks** to influence a decision, such as the selection of a service provider or the use of certain investments. The temptations of money have often led people astray.

The IRS adds other provisions for enforcement, such as nondiscrimination testing. Highly compensated employees must not be allowed to defer a much higher percentage of their paycheck than non–highly compensated employees. Generally, they can defer only two percentage points more on average. Likewise, the employer contributions cannot be far higher for the highly compensated employees. The IRS has formulas to define who is considered highly compensated and to determine whether the deferrals and contributions are within the range. The testing must be done annually unless the plan is exempted because of its safe-harbor status. It's important for the plan to stay in compliance with the IRS because the penalties, in severe cases, can include disqualification of the plan, a painful process for all involved.

THE THREAT OF LAWSUITS

A bigger source of potential legal liability for plan fiduciaries are lawsuits brought by plan participants. A large and growing number of high-profile lawsuits have been filed against plan fiduciaries in recent years. To illustrate the growth in fiduciary lawsuits, more than a hundred new 401(k) lawsuits were filed in 2016–17, the highest two-year total since the initial wave of lawsuits began in 2008–09.[12]

Generally, these suits revolve around excessive plan fees, both investment fees and fees from plan service providers, and the dollar amounts involved can be substantial. The Center for Retirement Research cited three main areas that are the basis of these lawsuits:[13]

- **Inappropriate investment choices.** This can include continuing to retain mutual funds that have a history of underperformance. This can also pertain to company stock that is included as an option that underperforms over time.
- **Excessive fees.** This can arise from plans offering high-cost retail share class funds when lower-cost share classes are available.

12 Alicia Munnell, "401(k) lawsuits are surging. Here's what it means for you," MarketWatch, May 12, 2018, https://www.marketwatch.com/story/401k-lawsuits-are-surging-heres-what-it-means-for-you-2018-05-09.

13 George Mellman and Geoffrey Sanzenbacher, "401(k) Lawsuits: What Are the Causes and Consequences?" Center for Retirement Research at Boston College, May 2018, https://crr.bc.edu/wp-content/uploads/2018/04/IB_18-8.pdf.

- **Self-dealing.** This refers to situations where fiduciaries use the plan or its assets to benefit themselves rather than the plan participants. Lawsuits have targeted investment firms that have kept their own products on the lineup even though those investments weren't performing well.

The suits brought by participants carry the potential for more significant financial repercussions than actions initiated by the DOL or IRS. In some cases, the DOL and IRS allow fiduciaries and sponsors that admit their mistakes the opportunity to self-correct with minimal monetary penalties. The lawsuits, by contrast, can become very costly. As a result, they have become, in effect, a significant enforcement mechanism as plans come into compliance out of fear of being sued. In that atmosphere, fiduciary committees have tended to become defensive-minded. Though that may be understandable, a better approach would be to focus on the desired outcome of providing a good plan, monitoring results, and living by the spirit of good fiduciary conduct.

COMMON MISTAKES THAT SPELL TROUBLE

If you and your colleagues adopt the attitude of doing what is best for the plan's participants, you are well on your way toward doing your duty as a plan fiduciary. Being familiar with the basic rules and working with an experienced ERISA attorney can prevent some common mistakes. Here are some examples of missteps that I see that can cause problems down the road:

- **Failing to document how decisions were made** and the process used. What factors were considered, and were outside experts consulted? In a lawsuit or a DOL investigation, one of the first questions is likely to be how the fiduciaries made their decisions. If the decision was four years ago, you will be far better off presenting the minutes of a meeting rather than stammering that you really don't remember.

- **Allowing the employer's interests to interfere** with doing what is in the best interests of the participants. This can be an outgrowth of an officer of the company being a member of the committee and not being able to differentiate the corporate role from the fiduciary duties. Even though company officers may be valuable as committee members, they must guard against the inherent conflict.
- **Conducting the committee's business informally.** Best practices include establishing a committee charter that governs member appointments, officer appointments including the chairperson, and meeting frequency. In my experience, only about 20 percent of committees operate formally, with written rules of procedure, a nominating panel, and terms of service. Establishing agendas and taking meeting minutes are an important way to show that the committee takes its work seriously. On our company's website, we offer a sample charter and agenda and a format for taking minutes of a meeting.

Know your responsibilities, take your job seriously, and document your decisions. Those three things will go a long way toward mitigating any potential liability.

THE BOTTOM LINE

- The best way for members of a fiduciary committee to keep a retirement plan out of legal trouble is knowing exactly what doing a good job requires—and then doing it.
- Lawsuits against defined-contribution plans were rare for the first quarter century that they existed. Today, they are common. Excessive fees have become the most prevalent complaint. Other issues often are inappropriate investment choices and self-dealing.
- The fiduciary committee must not play amateur lawyer. It needs to hire an attorney dedicated to the best interests of plan participants. The committee should ensure that the attorney represents their interests—not just the employer's interests.
- ERISA does not require fiduciary liability insurance, but committee members should insist on it—or get written indemnification from the employer.
- Plan fiduciaries could face federal fines and penalties for failing to meet ERISA standards. They must operate the plan exclusively to benefit participants and beneficiaries.
- The threat of lawsuits has led to better compliance but also has created an attitude of defensiveness on fiduciary committees. The best defense is to stay focused on providing a good plan and live by the spirit of the fiduciary standards.
- To avoid trouble, a fiduciary committee should conduct its business formally, document how it makes decisions, and refuse to put the employer's interests ahead of the participants' interests.

CHAPTER 5

CONDUCTING THE ORCHESTRA

From the perspective of plan participants, investing in a 401(k) or 403(b) often feels as if they don't have to give the matter much thought. Somewhere along the line, they likely signed an enrollment form to withhold 5 or 10 percent from their paychecks. Every so often, they pull up a website or glance at a quarterly report and see how much money they have.

Simple, right? For that to happen, though, a lot of people must cooperate. The enrollment form goes to human resources, which sends it to payroll, where someone updates the file. Someone else calculates the employer match, then they add instructions to divvy up the contributions between the accounts that the employee has selected from the investment lineup.

Then, every time money is withheld, it goes to the custodian, who within a day or two places the trades into the selected funds. At the same time, the plan recordkeeper is notified as to how much went where. The recordkeeper and the custodian link up, and the dollar tallies show up in the participant's account on the website.

At the end of the year, an auditor examines a sampling of those deposits to ensure they were accurate and timely and the right match was applied. The plan adviser looks over the accounts to discern whether the employees are on pace for retirement. An attorney weighs in on questions such as what constitutes the total compensation on which the deferral percentage is calculated.

As you can see, every dollar flowing through the system gets the attention of a lot of people—and if anyone doesn't do his or her job, or they communicate poorly, the process can break down quickly. And that's where the fiduciary committee comes in—to make sure that all parties act responsibly. When they do, it all comes together to make what is exceedingly complex seem so deceptively simple.

THE RETIREMENT PLAN ENSEMBLE

For an orchestra to fill a concert hall with harmonies, the musicians each must know their part and get the timing just right, paying close attention to the conductor. As a fiduciary who is responsible for managing your organization's retirement plan, you are the conductor.

One of your most important duties is to assemble the right players. This entails both working with internal company resources and hiring outside vendors. You need to ask yourself two questions about the talent that you assemble:

- What did you hire them to do?
- How do you know they are doing a good job?

In this chapter, we will introduce the following members of your fiduciary ensemble: the plan adviser, the recordkeeper, the custodian, the ERISA attorney, the plan auditor, and the internal staff.

THE PLAN ADVISER

While all those professionals play central roles, I believe that the plan adviser is perhaps the most important hire you will make as a fiduciary. The plan adviser can be considered the first chair of the group. That is because of the impact on the plan's performance and the adviser's ability to recommend other service providers, such as the ERISA attorney, recordkeeper, and custodian, based on their experience and knowledge of the industry.

The adviser's most visible function is to aid you in establishing the investment lineup and monitoring those investments. The adviser provides guidance on the asset classes and specific funds to include within those classes. That is a key role, considering that the performance of the fund lineup greatly influences the retirement security of the participants.

An effective plan adviser puts more money in the participants' pockets, which compounds significantly over a working career and adds to their retirement readiness.

The plan adviser should also help you and your colleagues to negotiate and monitor the fees that the plan pays to the other service providers. Those fees also have a major influence on the participant's ability to accumulate money over their career. Advisers specializing in 401(k)s and 403(b)s typically have comprehensive benchmarks that you can use to compare the fees. Just as investment performance directly benefits the participants, so does each dollar saved in fees.

In those ways, an effective plan adviser puts more money in the participants' pockets, which compounds significantly over a working career and adds to their retirement readiness. Retirement readiness depends on a variety of factors, such as the terms of the plan, including automatic enrollment and escalation, which we will discuss in chapter 8. The most important factor is the participant's consistent and substantial contributions. Once those contributions are in place, the investment performance and plan fees have a major influence on the compounding effect.

The plan adviser will also typically offer participant enrollment and education services. More on that in chapters 7 and 8.

Be sure to select a plan adviser without any conflict of interest that could sway their recommendations—for example, a compensation arrangement with an outside fund company or investment manager. This includes accepting upfront commissions or so-called trailing commissions such as 12b-1 fees. The only compensation that plan advisers should receive is from the fees paid for services to the plan.

Conflicts of interest are rampant in the plan adviser industry, harming countless plans and participants. The financial media have spread the news about the need for fee-only financial advisers for individual investors, but that awareness hasn't extended to participants in 401(k)s and 403(b)s. It would be refreshing to hear talk of fee-only plan advisers for retirement plans who accept no commissions or other self-serving compensation—nothing but a clearly stated fee.

Commonly, for example, a plan adviser will receive substantial marketing payments from an investment manager (i.e., a company that manages and sells mutual funds) to get prospects in the door. If the plan adviser gets new clients, the investment manager gets more money in its mutual funds. Receiving those marketing payments creates a conflict for the plan adviser, who is now relying upon the payments to generate client growth. Or the investment manager will sponsor a conference or a due-diligence trip to some exotic locale, which amounts to a four-day junket with the mutual fund companies footing the bill. Plan advisers who are representatives of larger firms, known as broker/dealer firms, often rely on them to create a preferred list of funds that they will then use to recommend to their clients. The presumption is that these are funds of proven excellence. The reality often is that these are funds of investment managers that have paid the broker/dealer large sums for the right to be on the list. These are often called pay-to-play arrangements.

Such practices are disgusting, frankly, yet they are more than common. They are the norm in my industry, flourishing in the shadows because nobody puts a spotlight on them. Ironically, plan advisers can accept dubious compensation and still call themselves fiduciaries. They can meet that definition in part by disclosing the various forms of compensation to the client—which they will do, somewhere in the depths of the mandatory disclosure document, Form ADV Part 2. The client gets a copy but rarely sees or understands the disclosure.

As a fiduciary for your organization's plan, refuse to hire an adviser who participates in those practices. You should outright ask. Find out exactly where any conflicts are disclosed. And watch for subtle influences too. If the plan adviser recommends a certain recordkeeper, for example, is that recordkeeper taking the adviser out to lunch now and then? Maybe that's no big deal. Does the recordkeeper invite the adviser to a weekend party every year? A big red flag. How about a payment of $10,000 a year in marketing money to help grow the adviser's business?

The influences become progressively intolerable. You should have no part of it. If your doctor writes you a prescription, you would like to presume you're getting the best medicine. Imagine finding out the pharmaceutical company was paying your doctor for each prescription written. Would you just shrug? At Pension Consultants, we prohibit our employees from accepting meals, travel, or anything. If someone mails us a package of golf balls, our policy is to mail it back.

A good plan adviser, free of conflict and experienced in the industry, can be a valuable resource and a true partner in helping you carry out your fiduciary responsibilities. Such advisers will share insights that you need when looking for the right qualities in a record-keeper, custodian, or other service provider.

Select only a plan adviser who accepts fiduciary responsibility in writing. Plan advisers can fall under one of two classes of fiduciary, based on the level of control over the investments:

- **A 3(21) adviser has a co-fiduciary role** in which the adviser provides the plan with advice on the investments offered and the overall lineup, but the committee retains discretion and makes the final decisions.

- **A 3(38) adviser has full discretion to make and implement fund and investment lineup decisions.** The committee offloads the fiduciary risk of asset class and fund selection to the adviser in this situation. Still, you and the committee will need to monitor how well the adviser performs and whether, if needed, to make a change. You cannot offload your oversight responsibility, nor the fact that you hired the adviser.

As with all vendors, you will need to monitor the fees paid to the plan adviser. You can do that by using a benchmark for what the typical adviser charges for a plan like yours. If for some reason the data for a benchmark comparison isn't available, you still need to verify that you are paying a reasonable amount. You can do so through a request for proposal, or RFP. More on that in chapter 7.

How do you know whether the plan adviser is doing a good job? I believe it comes down to this: the lineup of investment choices will be performing well; the fees paid by the plan will be low; and the participants will be making sufficient contributions to be on pace for retirement. Those are the three key metrics that are central to the success of your plan, and we will explore each of them in upcoming chapters.

THE RECORDKEEPER

The plan's recordkeeper is in charge of the tracking and reporting of participants' accounts as well as conducting the nondiscrimination testing for the plan. Those are the core services of the recordkeeper.

In a small plan, the recordkeeper often is an independent local third-party administrator, or TPA. In larger plans, the recordkeeping function likely will be performed by a national provider that is partnered with a custodian. Those national providers also will likely offer many ancillary services, such as participant enrollment and participant education and advice. Those services may or may not be a good fit for your plan.

Accurately tracking the amount of money in each participant's account and the vesting status is an obviously crucial function and a complicated task. Consider the potential sources of money in each participant's account, including:

- salary deferral contributions
- employer matching contributions
- profit-sharing contributions
- earnings on investments
- fees paid from plan assets apportioned to participant accounts

- forfeiture payments allocated to participant accounts
- rollover contributions into the plan

The recordkeeper also typically prepares the annual Form 5500 filing for the plan, using the financial information and statements generated by the plan's outside auditor. This is a required informational return for most plans.

Last and certainly not least, reporting is one of the most important functions of the recordkeeper. This includes the preparation of quarterly participant statements, as well as the daily valuation needed for accurate participant account information via the plan's web portal.

You will know that the recordkeeper is doing a good job based upon accuracy, timeliness, and service. Your benefits team or HR team, which works closely with the recordkeeper, will be the best source for assessing performance. And again, as with all providers, regularly benchmark the fees or periodically conduct an RFP to be confident that you are getting a good deal for your participants.

THE CUSTODIAN

The plan's custodian—generally an investment firm, trust company, or bank—is responsible for holding the plan's assets. The custodian often acts as a directed trustee, executing transactions only if directed to do so. Custodians have a fiduciary duty but not discretionary authority over those assets.

The 401(k) or 403(b) participants will make regular contributions to their investments and may occasionally make trades. The custodian also will receive instructions periodically regarding distributions to participants or changes in the investment lineup.

Even though thousands of participants may invest in a particular fund in the lineup, the custodian holds only one account per fund. As a result, the recordkeeper and custodian must maintain a close partnership. For example, the money from all participants invested in ABC fund is held in only one account at the custodian. That investment account's daily valuation is shared with the recordkeeper, who must keep track of how much each participant owns of that account. Their systems then reflect the current value for each participant.

You hire a custodian/directed trustee to safeguard the assets of the plan. To determine whether the custodian is doing a good job, make sure that part of the internal staff is responsible for reviewing the custodian's statements, comparing them to your records for timeliness and accuracy of deposits. The plan's auditor is the primary check on the custodian's accuracy.

THE ERISA ATTORNEY

As we discussed in chapter 4, it is critical that the committee engage the services of a knowledgeable, experienced ERISA attorney who understands both applicable law and regulations. Those insights are invaluable to you as a fiduciary. Some fiduciary committees simply rely on the plan adviser or recordkeeper, who may have an attorney or a compliance professional on staff, but the best practice is to hire independent counsel.

Questions commonly arise regarding situations that are specific to a participant or group of participants. For example, if the company terminates an employee who receives severance money, should a deferral be withheld from that pay? Is it compensation? Such questions call for a lawyer's expertise. The ERISA attorney you choose should be available to your internal staff in HR, payroll, and benefits as needed to answer their questions and to ensure that the administration of the plan goes smoothly.

The ERISA attorney's job is to guide the fiduciary committee to keep the administration of the plan in compliance and protected from governmental regulators and lawsuits. You will know the attorney is doing a good job if he or she is actively engaged with internal staff and reports frequently to the fiduciary committee, giving you confidence that the plan and its management comply with current law and regulations.

As you strive to save costs for the participants, review the attorney's fees periodically, as you should do with all fees paid by the plan. If you are unsure whether your ERISA attorney's fees are fair and reasonable, conduct an RFP. Managing expenses and overseeing the work of all the service providers is your obligation.

THE PLAN AUDITOR

ERISA requires an annual audit of most plans with a hundred or more participants at the beginning of the plan year. A qualified public accountant must conduct the audit, which must be submitted each year with the Form 5500 annual report to the Department of Labor. The plan auditor should have extensive experience with employee benefit plans. Do not hire an auditor that has worked with only a few plans.

The primary purpose of the annual audit is to protect the assets of the plan. To that end, the auditor will evaluate the strength of the plan's internal controls over the financial reporting. The audit can uncover administrative shortfalls, including operational errors and prohibited transactions, so that you can take corrective action.

According to the DOL's Employee Benefits Security Administration, after the audit has been completed, you should ask your plan auditor these questions:

- Were the plan assets fairly reported?
- Were the plan obligations properly stated and described?
- Were contributions properly calculated and received on time?
- Did the plan pay benefits in accordance with its terms?
- Were employees properly included or excluded from participating?
- Were the participant accounts fairly stated?
- Did the audit identify issues that could impact the plan's tax status?
- If any prohibited transactions were found, were they properly reported?

You will know whether the auditor is doing a good job if you get thorough answers to those questions and the audit meets the annual deadline to be filed with Form 5500. Also ask your ERISA attorney about the audit's thoroughness.

As always, review the fees charged to the plan. Compare the auditor's fees to an appropriate benchmark, and, if necessary, conduct an RFP.

DUTIES OF THE INTERNAL STAFF

Internal staff is critical to the successful operation and administration of a 401(k) or 403(b) plan. Depending upon the structure of your organization, the human resources, benefits, and payroll departments will all play crucial roles.

The fiduciary committee's oversight of internal staff members can feel awkward. You are responsible for overseeing how they administer the retirement plan, and if something goes wrong you must address it. That can take finesse, since the staff might not recognize your authority to tell them how to do their job. If they make a mistake, they might report it to their supervisor and you might never hear about it. That awkwardness can be eased if the benefits or HR director is a member of your committee or if the director regularly attends your meetings to explain and clarify the processes. Ask for periodic reports from the departments on how they are functioning, including any problems or errors.

The internal staff typically handles basic administrative functions such as these:

- Determining when participants are eligible and ensuring that newly eligible participants are enrolled in the plan.
- Processing employee deferrals and ensuring they are correctly deposited into the participant's account in a timely fashion.
- Updating deferral rates when participants make a change.
- Sending all required notices to plan participants.
- Approving and processing distributions, rollovers, and QDRO payouts.
- Processing benefits and payouts for terminated employees.

Specifically, HR and payroll are on the front lines of dealing with the plan participants to ensure that their deferrals are processed and handled correctly. You will know that the internal staff members are doing a good job if eligible participants are enrolled on time, contributions are deposited quickly and accurately, and the plan is administered consistent with the terms and conditions defined in the plan's documents.

PERFORMING IN HARMONY

As you evaluate your service providers, remember those two primary questions: *What did you hire them to do? How do you know if they are doing a good job?* Revisit those questions regularly. Are those specialists and advisers helping in the way that you envisioned when you hired them? Are they making your task of running the plan easier or more difficult?

Also review how your organization's staff members administer the plan and execute their various roles. Are things running smoothly? If there are recurring problems, what can you, as plan fiduciaries, do to help? You may need to ensure that all lines of communication are appropriately open, and you may need to arrange for some staff members to get additional training on their roles.

As the conductor of the retirement plan ensemble, your job is to make sure that all the players are hitting the right notes. If everyone is playing from the same sheet and working in harmony, you can make beautiful music together.

THE BOTTOM LINE

- The fiduciary committee must hire qualified service providers at a reasonable price and ensure they act responsibly. They include the plan adviser, recordkeeper, custodian, ERISA attorney, and plan auditor.
- An experienced plan adviser who is free of conflicts of interest can be a true partner to the fiduciary committee in carrying out its duties. The adviser has a major impact on the plan's performance and can help the committee choose other service providers and negotiate their fees.
- Conflicts of interest are almost universal in the plan adviser industry. Many advisers accept perks from investment managers in exchange for peddling their funds.
- A plan adviser should provide written acceptance of fiduciary responsibility—either as a 3(21) adviser who recommends funds to the committee or a 3(38) adviser to whom the committee grants full discretion over the fund lineup.
- A qualified recordkeeper is essential for tracking each participant's account holdings, reporting daily valuations, and preparing quarterly statements. The recordkeeper may offer other services that may or may not be a good fit for the retirement plan.
- The plan's custodian safeguards the plan's assets and executes transactions as directed. The custodian works closely with the recordkeeper to calculate daily how much each participant owns of the funds on the investment menu.
- An experienced ERISA attorney who understands benefits law and its changes is an indispensable member of the fiduciary team. The fiduciary committee should have its

own lawyer who doesn't also serve the plan adviser or the recordkeeper.

- A plan auditor conducts the required annual review that must be submitted to the Department of Labor. The auditor evaluates the plan's strength and can uncover errors and prohibited transactions. Hire an auditor that has extensive experience with employee benefit plans.
- The fiduciary committee is responsible for overseeing how internal staff in the human resources, benefits, and payroll departments administer the retirement plan. That can be awkward if the staff doesn't recognize the committee's authority.

CHAPTER 6

WHAT'S ON THE MENU?

For those first five years, your anniversary was a big deal. You never failed to come up with something good. Then came year six—and nothing. It was downhill from there. That five-year track record didn't seem to count for much now. Let's just say that past performance is no guarantee of future success.

We're talking about investment management here, not marriage, though they do have some things in common. You go into each hopefully with a set of expectations and vulnerabilities—and you must remain attentive if you want many happy returns.

In marriage, however, a proven performer likely will keep up the good work for another five years, and another. In the realm of investments, specifically in the selection of funds (commonly referred to as manager selection), it doesn't always work that way. A stretch of good years is often followed by a stretch of disappointing ones.

Such can be the cycle of fund performance: if a fund has been treating you well for a while, something's up—or rather, something soon could be down. That's why you shouldn't put all your faith in a fund's track record. You might not recognize when it's about to go south.

It seems counterintuitive, but the successful selection of funds can sometimes be the result of investing with them after they have experienced hard times. The losers may become winners once more, so long as they are fundamentally sound. Wise investors keep an open mind and proceed cautiously. Whether for love or money, only fools rush in.

It's human nature, in large part. Shiny objects mesmerize us. Investors, particularly amateurs, naturally want to get in on the action and place their bets on the rising stars, the funds du jour. What they do not always realize is that by the time they hear all the hoopla, those stars may have gone about as high as they will go. Every star that rises also sets—and that's the way it always has been in the investment world.

Unfortunately, it's not just the amateurs who get blinded by the light. Money managers and advisers of all stripes, whether they are investing on behalf of individuals, mutual funds, or retirement plans, often make the same mistake. That's partly because of the capricious nature of investment securities, but it's also partly due to the salesy nature of many of the people who peddle investments of various kinds. For fiduciary committees, the investments to be selected are usually mutual funds. Most funds are sold, and it's easiest to sell the ones that are currently showing an impressive track record. The buyer sees the returns that have been posted over the last year, or three years, or five years, and *wow*!

Inevitably, the fund's performance may begin to slip. At first, the strong track record covers that fact, and the investment still shows favorable long-term results. A faltering return in one-quarter of the year has little impact on the one-year record and even less on the three- and five-year returns. To the investor, the fund can still look golden, and so does the adviser who recommended it. "Look here," the adviser says, pointing at a graph. "We're good."

Fiduciary committees for retirement plans tend to figure that their investment professionals know best. The plan adviser recommends a great fund and touts its track record. Invariably, the committee nods in approval. A year or so later, that fund's performance is eroding. Once that downward trend becomes apparent and the track record clearly reflects it, the adviser recommends a different star that has reached its zenith—and before long this new one, too, is fading.

In other words, fund selection decisions often amount to getting in high, pulling out low, and repeating. That's common among individual investors, as study after study has shown, and it's common among retirement plan advisers and the fiduciary committees that hire them. It's not exactly an effective way to enhance the performance for the plan participants, and yet time and time again it happens.

In my experience, whenever our firm begins working with a new client, the fiduciaries lack a clear idea of how their funds have performed for their participants. They only know that they have routinely reviewed the track records for the various funds and that the plan adviser notifies them when a fund has lost its shine. Because of a sad lack of transparency, they do not see what truly is happening.

The reason this is so important is because the participants don't get to invest in the fund before it was selected or after it was removed. The participant's portfolio performance is determined by the fund's performance only while it is on the menu.

Frankly, many plan advisers as well as financial advisers who serve individuals have little incentive to reveal how they have performed personally for their clients in their fund selection. They have little interest in discovering their own track record too, because such knowledge would likely only underscore their inability to do so effectively. It is an open secret in the investment industry. Most advisers simply aren't very good at fund selection. They are primarily valued by the investment firms that offer funds for getting business and keeping business.

I am proud to say that Pension Consultants Inc. doesn't take that approach. We track our fund selection performance and report it each quarter to our clients. Across the board, fiduciary committees need more of that transparency. In the Mizzou study that we commissioned, only 32 percent of plans in 2013, 12 percent in 2014, and 30 percent in 2015 of the 401(k)s that it examined had generated a performance any better than the all-index menu benchmark that we recommend. A subsequent update to the study found that 11 percent beat the benchmark in 2016 and 83 percent did in 2017. Why has poor fund selection performance been tolerated by fiduciary committees? Because it is never reported to them.

YOUR INVESTMENT LINEUP

A critical component of a good 401(k) or 403(b) plan is an investment lineup that performs well. The return made on an investment compounds powerfully over time. Since helping the participants accumulate enough money for a secure retirement is the ultimate objective of the plan, investment performance must be addressed.

You can be confident that your plan's investment menu is performing well when it outperforms an all-index lineup, net of investment fees. In this chapter, you will discover how to know whether your plan is reaching that goal. The point isn't to transform you or the fiduciary committee into stock traders or hedge fund managers. It is simply to empower you to judge the performance of those who advise you in this important area.

You can be confident that your plan's investment menu is performing well when it outperforms an all-index lineup, net of investment fees.

When compounded over time, even a seemingly small difference in return can have a profound impact on the amount of money that participants can accumulate for their retirement. To illustrate, let's look at the impact over a thirty-five-year career of a 5.5 percent annual return versus returns of 6.0 and 6.5 percent. Here are the assumptions:

- Participant age thirty
- Works for thirty-five more years
- Annual salary is $50,000, with an annual 2 percent increase in salary
- Contributes 10 percent of salary
- Employer will match 50 percent on up to 6 percent of salary

	AMOUNT ACCUMULATED OVER 35 YEARS	DIFFERENCE VS. 5.5%
5.5% average return	$863,071	NA
6.0% average return	$953,769	+10.5%
6.5% average return	$1,055,689	+22.3%

As you can see, a small improvement in annual returns can make a large impact on the accumulated account balance of one person.

Multiply that difference by the total number of your plan's participants, and the dollar amounts become very large. That's why an investment lineup that performs well is so critical. It will make a major difference for the coworkers you serve.

Very likely, your plan already has an investment lineup. Typically, today's plans offer ten to twenty selections—although in the early days of 401(k)s some offered fifty or more, which many participants found to be overwhelming and so simply chose the first few listed. You and the other fiduciaries on the plan committee don't have to start from scratch. But, to get the right perspective, it's important to understand how investment lineups are assembled.

START WITH ASSET CLASSES

When building an investment lineup for a plan, your starting point should be the asset classes to be used. An asset class is a category of investment. For example, the broadest asset classes are cash, fixed income (bonds), and equities (stocks). Further subdividing these broad asset classes results in narrower groupings such as government bonds, corporate bonds, large stocks, small stocks, etc. An asset class, therefore, is simply a grouping of investments with similar qualities.

The employees who participate in the plan will have a variety of investing needs. They will have a wide range of ages and varying tolerance for risk, and they will have accumulated differing amounts for retirement. Some will have more investing experience than others and be more comfortable with managing their own accounts.

One of the challenges of building an investment lineup is to offer a sufficient number of asset classes to satisfy the needs of the range of participants without offering so many choices that participants are intimidated, or even paralyzed, by the number of choices.

We typically include the following asset classes in the plans we work with:

ASSET CLASS
Cash
Intermediate Government Bond
Corporate Bond
High-Yield Bond
Target Date (allocation) Series
Large-Value Stock
Large-Growth Stock
Mid-Value Stock
Mid-Growth Stock
Small-Value Stock
Small-Growth Stock
Foreign Large-Blend Stock
Diversified Emerging Markets
Real Estate

SETTING YOUR STANDARDS

After selecting the asset classes, you need a benchmark for each. The benchmarks will provide a basis to judge their performance.

Benchmarking is important because investment performance is always relative. For example, if your investment earned a return of 14 percent in a year, would you consider that good? Most people immediately say yes. But what if other investments similar to yours earned an average of 16 percent that year? Or imagine that your investment lost 4 percent for the year. Most people immediately think something is wrong—but if similar investments lost 7 percent in the same time period, your investment actually performed very well. Without a benchmark, you cannot judge how well your investment performed compared to others.

The benchmarks for each asset class should set a high but fair standard. The standard should not be set so low as to become meaningless, nor so high that it likely will be unattainable and meaningless as well. The standard also should be objective and measurable.

INDEXES MAKE GOOD BENCHMARKS

So what is the appropriate standard of performance for benchmarking the asset classes? The answer is an index—a separate one for each asset class. An index consists of a hypothetical portfolio of securities designed to represent a particular segment of the market. One of the best known is the Standard & Poor's 500. Since indexes have been developed that represent most asset classes, they often are used as benchmarks.

You cannot invest directly in an index. It is only a comparison tool. However, an entire industry of mutual funds closely tracks the performance of various indexes. These are called index funds. An example would be the popular Vanguard 500 Index fund (ticker symbol VFIAX), which closely mirrors the S&P 500 index.

Since they are unmanaged on a day-to-day basis, index funds are often referred to as passive. By contrast, an active fund has a manager who chooses investments that are expected to perform well and who sells those that are expected to do poorly.

Research has shown that most active fund managers fail to outperform their benchmark index. CNBC recently cited a study by index provider S&P that reinforces the underperformance of active managers versus their benchmarks for the ten years ending December 31, 2018:

- Large-cap managers: 85.1% underperformed their benchmark.
- Small-cap managers: 85.7% underperformed their benchmark.
- Mid-cap managers: 88.0% underperformed their benchmark.

The report states, "Over long-term horizons, 80 percent or more of active managers across all categories underperformed their respective benchmarks."

There are two important takeaways for you and the fiduciary committee.

1. The appropriate benchmark for each asset class is an index.
2. An actively managed fund should only be chosen to fill an asset class if you are confident that it will outperform its index benchmark. Otherwise, an index fund is the better choice.

This is not to say that active managers should be dismissed out of hand, but rather there needs to be a compelling reason to go with an active manager over an index fund. Though it is difficult to find them, active managers who do beat their index benchmarks are very valuable.

If you go back to the first table in this chapter, imagine that the benchmark index provided the 6 percent return. Active fund managers who could outperform and make a 6.5 percent return, in this example, contribute significant value to the investors over time. However, a 5.5 percent return, or anything less than the benchmark, would be unacceptable.

Now, let's go back to our fund lineup. The chart now includes the asset classes mentioned along with the index benchmarks that we use for our clients.

ASSET CLASS *BENCHMARK*
Cash *3-month T-Bill*
Intermediate Government Bond *Bbg US MBS TR USD*
Corporate Bond *Bbg US Credit TR USD*
High-Yield Bond *Bbg US Corp High-Yield TR USD*
Target Date (allocation) *S&P Target Date through Series TR USD*
Large-Value *Russell 1000 Value TR USD*
Large-Growth *Russell 1000 Growth TR USD*
Mid-Value *Russell Mid-Cap Value TR USD*
Mid-Growth *Russell Mid-Cap Growth TR USD*
Small-Value *Russell 2000 Value TR USD*
Small-Growth *Russell 2000 Growth TR USD*
Foreign Large-Blend *MSCI EAFE NR USD*
Diversified Emerging Markets *MSCI EM NR USD*
Real Estate *MSCI US REIT GR USD*

A FUND FOR EACH ASSET CLASS

After settling on a list of asset classes and benchmarks, the next step is to select one fund to represent each asset class (or, in the case of target date funds, a series of funds in five-year increments to represent the progression toward retirement). This is manager selection.

Manager selection is a difficult task. Again, most active funds do not beat their index benchmark over long time periods. Nonetheless, the goal for each asset class is to select a manager (i.e., fund) that will outperform the benchmark over time. To avoid selecting an underperforming fund requires professional judgment—and even then, there is no guarantee of success.

No doubt, you will rely heavily upon the plan adviser, who should use various metrics, attributes, and experience. The adviser should consider many aspects of the firm and its management team.

Here are a few of the many things we look for when selecting a fund manager:

- **Specialization of the firm:** If you are looking for a large-cap value manager, choose a company dedicated entirely to the value style of investing, not growth. For international securities, choose a firm specializing in them, not one that just includes an international fund among many other offerings.
- **Depth of research staff:** With all else being equal, choose a fund manager with a dozen or more researchers on staff rather than just two or three. The quality of the research correlates directly to the quality of the stocks and bonds selected.
- **Concentration of the portfolio's holdings:** A fund that has only forty or fifty stock holdings has more confidence and conviction in its choices than a fund with a few hundred. Too many holdings indicates that the fund is guarding against bad

judgment. It ends up replicating the index that it is supposed to be beating.

- **Compensation structure of the management team:** The management team should have enough of a financial incentive to outperform the benchmark index.
- **Expense ratio:** The lower the fund's expenses, the more likely it is to outperform a similar fund with higher expenses. In study after study, the expense ratio has the strongest correlation to performance.

The purpose in selecting funds is not to identify those that have outperformed in the past. That's easy to do in a few moments with a database and spreadsheet. The purpose is to identify the future outperformers. In other words, choose a fund manager not for what they did but for what they will do. That's so obvious that people lose sight of it. They continue to look at the fund's track record even after buying it.

Choose a fund manager not for what they did but for what they will do.

At Pension Consultants, we look at past performance to find managers that have a strong long-term track record but recently may have fallen out of cycle and out of favor. That can be a good time to acquire them and enjoy the ride back up. That might seem like common sense, but people tend to invest emotionally—and the industry, which has a strong sales and marketing culture, encourages that. The fund companies advertise most heavily when their offerings are at their peak performance. Investors see the rave reports in popular financial magazines, for example, and scramble to get their shares. They buy high, and they often end up selling low in their disappointment.

Each fund's performance should be measured net (after the deduction) of all investment-related fees. When mutual funds are used, the investment returns should already be shown net of the fund's expense ratio.

If your plan uses something different than mutual funds (i.e., separate accounts or collective trusts), you will need to understand whether returns are stated before or after fees to be sure the committee is reviewing the investment's performance correctly.

Now let's go back to our chart of asset classes and add hypothetical names of the chosen funds.

ASSET CLASS / BENCHMARK	FUND NAME
Cash *3-month T-Bill*	Money Market Fund ABC
Intermediate Government Bond *Bbg US MBS TR USD*	DEF Intermediate Government Fund A
Corporate Bond *Bbg US Credit TR USD*	GHI Core Bond Fund
High-Yield Bond *Bbg US Corp High-Yield TR USD*	Gwynda's HY Bond Fund
Target Date (allocation) *S&P Target Date through Series TR USD*	Stephanie's Target Date Series 1-5
Large-Value *Russell 1000 Value TR USD*	Zach's Large-Value Fund
Large-Growth *Russell 1000 Growth TR USD*	Jake's Large-Growth Fund
Mid-Value *Russell Mid-Cap Value TR USD*	Rachel's Mid-Value Fund
Mid-Growth *Russell Mid-Cap Growth TR USD*	Mary's Mid-Growth Fund
Small-Value *Russell 2000 Value TR USD*	Judah's Small-Value Fund

Small-Growth *Russell 2000 Growth TR USD*	Henry's Small-Growth Fund
Foreign Large-Blend *MSCI EAFE NR USD*	Zoe's Foreign Fund
Diversified Emerging Markets *MSCI EM NR USD*	123 Emerging Market Fund
Real Estate *MSCI US REIT GR USD*	A1 Real Estate Fund

The takeaways are:

1. The fund is selected to fill the asset class. That is, to stay true to the asset class.
2. The fund is selected with the expectation that it will match or exceed the benchmark performance over time.

EVALUATING YOUR LINEUP

Now that we have selected the asset classes, the funds, and the benchmarks, we are ready to begin tracking the performance of the lineup. The objective is to show the performance of the funds that were available to the participants. In other words, for the time the funds were in the lineup, how did they perform versus their benchmarks? These are the results of the manager selection decisions.

It might seem obvious to measure the performance of the funds while they are available to the participants via the investment menu. The participants, after all, can only earn investment returns on the funds while they are in the lineup. Fund performance before or after their inclusion on the menu is meaningless to them. But the meaningful performance is rarely calculated.

This process will not tell us how or why we selected the funds.

That is the judgment usually left to the plan adviser. For each fund, for each asset class, the plan adviser will either make the selection (as a 3(38) investment manager) or make a recommendation to the committee (as a 3(21) adviser). The process by which advisers make their selection or recommendation is outside the purview of this book.

However, you shouldn't just blindly trust the plan adviser without ever knowing if the selections or recommendations contributed to, or detracted from, the overall performance of the plan lineup. Measuring the lineup's performance as outlined will allow your committee to illuminate the value of your adviser's judgment over time.

I believe that once a fund is included in the investment lineup, its past performance becomes irrelevant when measuring the lineup's performance. Yes, that's right—irrelevant. That is because the only performance that matters to the participants—and to your committee—is how well the fund does moving forward now that it is in the lineup.

This means, for purposes of measuring the performance of the lineup, that we will no longer look at the impressive track records of the funds prior to their addition into the lineup. That will give a much truer picture of the performance that the plan participants experience.

DEALING WITH FUND CHANGES

Periodically, the plan adviser will change one of the funds in the lineup or suggest a fund change to the committee. This is often the result of poor fund performance relative to its benchmark or for other reasons, such as turnover in the management of the fund.

Again, the new fund's performance should only count once it is in place. Its past performance doesn't matter anymore. However, the old fund's performance cannot simply be disregarded. You can't just toss it aside and pretend it never existed. It still influenced the performance of the fund lineup for the time it was there.

Therefore, you must keep track of how well the old fund did during the time that your plan offered it. That will be essential information for evaluating how well your plan adviser has performed for you. The adviser may not like that approach. It may make the adviser look bad. Therefore, your committee may need to insist on this method of reporting, or you may need to do the tracking yourself.

KNOWING YOUR NUMBERS

In benchmarking the lineup as a whole, we suggest equally weighting the performance of each asset class. As plan fiduciaries, you have no control over how the participants allocate their money, so the equal weighting will provide an overall figure for comparison.

Here's how to do that calculation for each time period:

1. Compare each fund's rate of return to that of its index benchmark. This assumes the fund was in the lineup for the entire time period.

2. For each, subtract the benchmark rate from the fund rate to find the difference, whether positive or negative.

3. Add up the differences to get a total.

This chart shows how that might look for a given period:[14]

14 Please understand that these are hypothetical figures that do not correlate to an actual plan's lineup performance. There is no guarantee that your investment lineup will result in any particular rate of return.

ASSET CLASS / BENCHMARK	PERIOD RETURN-FUND	PERIOD RETURN-BENCHMARK	OUTPERFORMANCE / (UNDERPERFORMANCE)
Cash *3-month T-Bill*	2.1%	2.0%	0.1
Intermediate Government Bond *Bbg US MBS TR USD*	2.9%	2.9%	0.0
Corporate Bond *Bbg US Credit TR USD*	2.3%	2.7%	(0.4)
High-Yield Bond *Bbg US Corp High-Yield TR USD*	2.9%	3.3%	(0.4)
Target Date (allocation) *S&P Target Date through Series TR USD*	7.8%	8.0%	(0.2)
Large-Value *Russell 1000 Value TR USD*	10.1%	9.9%	0.2
Large-Growth *Russell 1000 Growth TR USD*	11.0%	10.8%	0.2
Mid-Value *Russell Mid-Cap Value TR USD*	13.9%	14.5%	(0.6)
Mid-Growth *Russell Mid-Cap Growth TR USD*	12.5%	12.1%	0.4
Small-Value *Russell 2000 Value TR USD*	10.2%	9.6%	0.6
Small-Growth *Russell 2000 Growth TR USD*	11.1%	10.8%	0.3
Foreign Large-Blend *MSCI EAFE NR USD*	9.8%	11.1%	(1.3)
Diversified Emerging Markets *MSCI EM NR USD*	11.3%	10.3%	1.0
Real Estate *MSCI US REIT GR USD*	6.6%	6.1%	0.5
Total			**0.4**

As the chart shows, the fund lineup as a whole outperformed the indexes as a whole.[15] (Note: for a target date fund series, we would use an equal-weighted aggregate of the funds within that series and of the benchmarks for each fund.)

HOW EFFECTIVE IS YOUR PLAN ADVISER?

How do funds perform *after* they are added to the lineup? That is the true measure of your plan's investment lineup and the value of your plan adviser. Unless you calculate the lineup performance as described, however, it is impossible to know whether the advice helped or hurt your participants.

When your committee begins tracking the performance of the investment lineup, you will naturally wonder about the time frame for making judgments about the plan adviser. A new adviser should get at least two years, perhaps three, before being assessed on manager selection performance. The first months or quarters are not enough time for that.

As a 3(38) investment manager, our firm fully owns the lineup's record for each plan we manage. We track our performance from the time we take control of the lineup. We call that time period "inception-to-date." Over time, we will develop a one-year record, three-year record, and so on for each client. But we always keep track of the inception-to-date performance. That is the ultimate impact we have made on the lineup's performance.

If your committee has a 3(21) investment adviser who recommends funds for your approval, you and the adviser will share the performance record. The recommendation is the adviser's responsibil-

15 Please understand that these are hypothetical figures that do not correlate to an actual plan's lineup performance. There is no guarantee that your investment lineup will result in any particular rate of return.

ity, but your committee still is responsible for accepting the recommendation and doing so in a timely manner.

Either way, with a 3(38) investment manager or a 3(21) investment adviser, your committee needs to know how the lineup is performing. Measuring the performance as I have described here is the only way to truly know—but it is virtually never done this way. Plan advisers tend to find such transparency threatening.

Nonetheless, this information is not difficult to compile. Once you make the simple calculations that I have described here, you will have a clear, precise picture of how well your investment lineup has performed and how well your adviser has chosen investments for your plan. Never forget your obligation to your fellow employees. They need good choices on the menu if they are to grow strong for retirement.

THE BOTTOM LINE

- Manager selection is the term for choosing the funds for the plan's lineup. It is very important to the performance that the participants ultimately achieve in their individual portfolio.
- Even a slight improvement in your investment lineup's performance, compounded over a working career, can dramatically improve the retirement readiness for the employees.
- The first step in building investment lineups is to decide upon the asset classes to include.
- Indexes are the best tool to benchmark the performance in those asset classes.
- A fund's track record matters when selecting it for the lineup. Once chosen, however, all that matters is how well it performs while it is available as a choice for the participants.
- By measuring how well funds perform only while in your lineup, you get a truer picture of how well your plan adviser has performed for you.
- The plan's investment lineup is performing well when it outperforms an all-index lineup, net of investment-related fees.

CHAPTER 7

WHY FEES MATTER

Jerry didn't know what to do.[16] He had decided to enroll in his company's retirement plan—but so many choices! Which of those funny-sounding funds would serve him best? The first two or three listed in the brochure? Maybe the ones his coworker Jim seemed to like? Jerry hadn't a clue. It hurt to think about it.

"I know just how you feel," Paul told him as they chatted at the enrollment meeting. The company had just named a plan adviser for its 401(k) plan, and Paul represented that firm. "You don't want to screw this up, man. This is your retirement we're talking about."

Jerry furrowed his brow. "Yeah," he said, "and this is all pretty

16 Please understand that these are hypothetical figures that do not correlate to an actual plan's lineup performance. There is no guarantee that your investment lineup will result in any particular rate of return.

new to me."

Paul put on a thoughtful look. "I tell you what, Jerry," he said, "you might be interested in our individual advice program."

"How's that work?"

"We'll just ask you some questions," Paul said, "to find out stuff like how much risk you're willing to take and how many years you can invest before you retire. We'll keep a watch over your account, and as you get older we'll show you the adjustments you need. You won't have to worry about a thing, Jerry. This will get you on the right track and keep you there. We'll take care of you."

Sounds good, Jerry thought. He asked around and found out that Jim, Patty, and Joe already had opted for the service. *Everyone's doing it*, he thought. *Must be a good deal, and it won't cost me all that much. And the company must believe it's the smart thing to do. After all, they brought these folks in.*

The fiduciary committee for Jerry's plan had heard the adviser's pitch, too, and liked the idea. "It's not as if this is some big expense for the plan or the employer," the rep explained. "Your people decide for themselves whether *they* want to pay. We'll meet with each one and explain why they should save more and how much. Wait and see, they'll be putting a whole lot more into the plan. You'll be helping them get in much better shape to retire when they should." The committee was impressed—because wasn't that what it's all about?

The plan adviser then set up those individual talks to walk the employees through the plan's enrollment and help them select the appropriate investment option. One of those decisions was whether to sign up for the customized advice service—*just a small fee of less than 1 percent, and with our expert guidance you could make that back and more!* Sure enough, 80 to 90 percent of them said yes.

The adviser proceeded to charge that percentage every year on the value of the account for each participant who signed up. In return, the adviser customized each account to the participant's unique circumstances and provided an annual report on progress toward retirement.

Jerry wanted help but hadn't realized what the program really would cost him. The fee would begin as a steady drip from his 401(k) account and turn into a bad leak. He would be shelling out hundreds of dollars annually, more and more as his savings grew. His costs would be more than that, though. The money no longer would be there to compound during his working days. Instead, it would be compounding for the plan adviser. Jerry's retirement savings would suffer significantly.

What he didn't understand, and what many retirement plan participants fail to understand, is the power of fees to erode an investment. Many of those charges, of course, are justified and essential for a plan to function. Some are questionable and unnecessary. All need to be examined. If excessive, fees can turn a comfortable retirement into a frugal one. And that's why they matter.

If excessive, fees can turn a comfortable retirement into a frugal one. And that's why they matter.

"NECESSARY AND REASONABLE"

The fiduciary committee decides which services are provided to the plan and its participants. This is a broad power and responsibility. With each service added, the committee will need to evaluate potential vendors and expenses.

ERISA provides general guidance to the committee in its Section 408(b)(2). There it states that to avoid running afoul of the statute's prohibited transaction provisions, the fiduciaries should furnish services that are *necessary* to the operation of the plan, while paying no more than *reasonable* compensation to the providers of those services.

Because each service costs money that often gets charged to the plan, the committee's decisions have major consequences for the plan's participants. Any fee paid by the plan is ultimately borne by the participants. Therefore, keeping those costs low is a vital aspect of a good plan.

In the previous chapter, we looked at investment performance after investment fees and expenses. The focus in this chapter will be on the fees associated with other plan services.

NEGATIVE RETURNS

Think of plan fees as negative investment returns. The fees that participants incur will reduce their balance available for retirement.

In chapter 6, we looked at a chart depicting returns over a thirty-five-year working career at different levels of average investment return.

	AMOUNT ACCUMULATED OVER 35 YEARS	DIFFERENCE VS. 5.5%
5.5% average return	$863,071	NA
6.0% average return	$953,769	+10.5%
6.5% average return	$1,055,689	+22.3%

As the chart indicates, investment returns compounded over a working career play a vital role in determining the amount of money a participant accumulates for retirement. Investment fees can significantly reduce that amount, but that's only part of the story. Other fees paid by the plan also impact participant balances.

In the following chart you can see the profound impact that a 1.0 percent difference in average annual net investment returns, combined with a 0.30 percent difference in annual plan expenses, can have on the ability of a participant to accumulate a sufficient retirement nest egg. The combination of lower investment returns with higher fees paid by the plan is significant.

NET AVERAGE INVESTMENT RETURN	ANNUAL PLAN EXPENSES	AMOUNT ACCUMULATED OVER 35 YEARS	DIFFERENCE VS. 0.50% IN PLAN EXPENSES AND 5.5% ANNUAL INVESTMENT RETURN
5.5% average return	0.50%	$783,305	NA
6.0% average return	0.35%	$889,182	+13.5%
6.5% average return	0.20%	$1,013,485	+29.2%

Together, the impact of investment performance and plan fees dramatically alters the retirement readiness of your employees. Lower expenses help participants retire on time. Higher fees eat away at their balances and how much their accounts can compound over the years. Every dime saved is, in essence, a dime added to their accounts—and that dime, invested for forty years at 6 percent, could turn into a dollar.

KEEPING IT SIMPLE

As a member of your plan's fiduciary committee, you will find many people coming forward who want to sell something. The plan you help oversee is valued in the millions. And money attracts all manner of people—some good, some not. It's an age-old tale. To keep fees low, therefore, your committee continually will confront the challenge of keeping the services offered to a necessary-only level.

For example, it is not uncommon for a recordkeeper to offer marketing campaigns targeting increased participation and deferrals. Many campaigns are elaborate with impressive graphics and materials, but are the results worth the cost to the plan? And, as you have seen, recordkeeping firms also often include days of individual participant education in a contract. It might seem like a great service, but often it goes unused. Someone else, such as the plan adviser, ends up doing it, or the service isn't requested every year.

To watch out for the participants, you should take every opportunity to lower the plan fees by cutting out unused or unnecessary services. Know what services you have authorized, and find out how much the fee would go down if you were to remove a service.

WATCH OUT FOR CONTRACT CHANGES

Be aware of notifications from vendors that change the contract terms, most of which can be altered with advance notice. Do you know who receives these communications? Is your fiduciary committee made aware of them?

Audit each vendor's charges. A quoted price isn't always the price paid, so compare the invoices to the expected price. If they differ, ask why. That may sound like busy work, but it isn't. Changes to contracts often go unnoticed, and charges do go up.

Your organization's internal staff members generally will be the ones who deal with the vendors on a regular basis. They receive the invoices and can do the comparisons, so as a fiduciary you should be asking them about those expenses. Sometimes the initial quotes never get referenced again. Don't let that happen. Most of the time, a staff member or two will sit in on committee meetings. They aren't voting members, typically, but they can answer your questions.

Reviewing fees should be a regular part of your committee's agenda. As part of our services, our firm does a fee analysis, comparing the invoices to the quoted price and also to the benchmarks for the services and how much similar plans pay.

In chapter 5, we examined the core services that vendors provide. Don't accept other services unless you have been apprised of exactly what will be provided and have determined that it is worth the cost to the participants. The vendors might prefer to keep things opaque, but transparency should be a requirement for doing business. If they want your business, they will come around to meeting your demand.

THE VENDOR'S FEE DISCLOSURE

"*Who's* on first, *What's* on second, *I Don't Know* is on third." If you're like me, you've chuckled more than once at that old Abbott and Costello routine about the ballplayers with the funny names. Abbott is less than forthright in explaining himself, leaving Costello confused and aggravated. It reminds me of how retirement plan vendors often explain their fees—and that's no laughing matter.

Every industry has its bad actors. Because so much money is invested in retirement plans, and because fiduciary committees typically are relatively unsophisticated, the environment is conducive to abuse, often in the form of unwarranted fees. Despite the necessary and reasonable provision of the original ERISA law, the abuse continued, so the DOL in 2012 issued a new regulation under that section.

The new regulation mandates that "covered service providers" to certain ERISA-governed plans also provide to the fiduciaries a clear disclosure of fees and what those fees are buying. Note that not all plans are covered by ERISA. If you work for the government, for example, or for a church, your retirement plan doesn't have to comply with ERISA. Under the original legislation, they were exempted from meeting the law's standards. The participants don't get the same protections. I served briefly on a police and firefighter pension board and was shocked at how poorly its defined-benefit plan was run.

Plan fiduciaries like yourself must be alert to any abuses and be faithful to protecting the employees who have so much to lose. In the Abbott and Costello routine, the shortstop's name is *I Don't Give a Darn*. Think of yourself as a shortstop, too—but you'd better care a great deal.

Here are some of the details and definitions under the Section 408(b)(2) regulation:

Covered service providers are those that reasonably expect to receive $1,000 or more in compensation, either directly or indirectly through an affiliate or another contractor. Covered service providers must give details about the services they will provide and the compensation that they expect.

Examples of covered service providers include:

- Any registered investment adviser (RIA) providing services to the plan or to the participants—think plan adviser.
- A plan fiduciary (as defined by ERISA) who provides a service to the plan, such as a trustee.
- Providers of brokerage or recordkeeping services, including those providing an investment platform.
- Other service providers who expect to receive indirect compensation.

Direct compensation, as defined by the DOL regulation, is paid directly to a service provider out of plan assets. It can also include compensation that the plan sponsor pays directly from company assets and later receives reimbursement from plan assets.

Indirect compensation includes fees paid to service providers from a variety of sources. The compensation might be from other plan service providers, revenue sharing arrangements from the investments offered in the plan, or a service provider platform. They might be in the form of commissions, finder's fees, or other soft dollar arrangements. The services could include accounting, auditing, actuarial, banking, consulting, custodial, insurance, investment advisory, legal, recordkeeping, securities brokerage, third-party administration, or valuation.

The 408(b)(2) fee disclosures are not standardized. The amount of detail varies from one vendor to the next. Still, they are an important tool for your committee to use in assessing services and fees. If you don't have those disclosures, request a copy from your vendors for reference. Also maintain records of disclosures from newly hired vendors or from an existing vendor's change in services or fees.

WILL THE EMPLOYER SHARE THE COSTS?

The fiduciary committee's next step should be to ask the employer to pay some (or all) of the fees. Employers aren't obligated to pay for the management of the plan, but many do—sometimes because that has long been their practice and the expense is in their budget every year. Employers pitch in to pay fees more often than you might imagine. It's not uncommon, for example, for the employer to pay the recordkeeper fee for the plan. Asking can't hurt.

Ordinarily, the committee has a fiduciary obligation to oversee the fees because the participants ultimately pay those fees. However, when the employer pays the plan's expenses, that is another matter entirely. If the employer pays for part of the services offered to the plan, the fiduciary obligation of the committee is removed for that part of the expense (unless the plan later reimburses the employer).

For example, let's say that the recordkeeping costs to your plan are $500,000 per year. If the employer pays half, the plan has only paid $250,000. The committee's fiduciary obligation is to determine whether $250,000 is a good deal, not $500,000. In this case, the participants likely are getting a great deal, thanks to the employer.

The key takeaway is that the fiduciary committee is primarily concerned with the fees paid by the plan. However, if the employer pays part of the operational expenses of the plan, the committee will still want to keep the overall fees low, even those paid by the employer. While it's not a fiduciary duty to help the employer reduce fees too, it's the right thing to do, considering the employer's generosity. The fiduciary committee also might choose to monitor any fees that the employer is paying. That's not required, but, again, it seems only right. Technically, the employer must oversee that portion of the fees, but probably isn't doing so, thinking the committee is taking care of that.

Until you ask, you won't know whether your employer will pay some of the plan fees. Maybe the employer will pay for the audit, or maybe the legal expenses or part of the recordkeeping. Just asking may be the quickest way to lower the fees paid by the plan.

BENCHMARKING THE SERVICE FEES

In the last chapter, we discussed benchmarking as a comparison tool for investment lineups. But benchmarking works for much more than investments. It is also a great tool for assessing plan fees.

Benchmarking requires enough data to calculate averages and other statistical metrics. For plan fees, a cottage industry has developed that gathers data on various plan services. Companies sell the data in various forms so that they can be sliced and diced into benchmarks of many forms. For example, what is the average recordkeeping fee for plans between $10 million and $20 million? Or what is the 25th percentile for fees of plans between five hundred participants and seven hundred fifty participants?

Some companies gather data on their own clients (for example, large recordkeepers such as Fidelity or Principal Financial Group). Others gather data through public documents such as the Form 5500 that provides details on retirement plan operations and finances. As a result, some benchmarks are worth more than others. For example, getting benchmark information about recordkeeping fees from your plan's recordkeeper isn't as valuable as receiving its information about auditors. When possible, use independent, third-party benchmark data.

REQUESTING A SPECIFIC PROPOSAL

If a reliable benchmark isn't available, or if you need a new vendor, your committee will want to conduct a request for proposal. An RFP differs from a benchmark in that it is based upon your plan's specific attributes. In effect, you are saying to the prospective vendors: "Here is our plan information and this is what we want. What services do you provide, and what do you charge?" As a result, the proposals you receive will be specific to your plan.

Assuming that your committee obtains a significant number of proposals, the data will be the best information to determine the market price for the services you seek. Unfortunately, an RFP is more time-consuming than a benchmark to administer and analyze. Its effectiveness also relies upon the specific companies that respond to the request. A small sample size isn't statistically reliable. The respondents might be three inferior plan advisers or four expensive recordkeepers.

An RFP also requires someone knowledgeable to draft it and interpret the responses. What information should be requested for auditors? What data is important to gather about plan advisers? Sometimes the committee itself drafts the RFP, or it asks its ERISA attorney to do it. The skill and experience of the author of the RFP will likely determine the quality of the responses. A poorly drafted RFP is unlikely to gather the information necessary to make a wise decision.

To stay out of legal trouble, some people in the industry suggest conducting an RFP for every service provider every three to five years. I see it differently. If you have a reliable benchmark, you probably don't need an RFP. For example, if your recordkeeper charges $125,000 a year, and you know that plans of similar size pay $150,000 a year for the same services, the benchmarking is your documentation that the costs are reasonable. The concept of an RFP sounds nice, but so much depends on who writes the proposal. It can illuminate good information, or it might not illuminate anything.

If you lack a good benchmark, then an RFP is a great tool. But when overused and poorly drafted, RFPs can become just busywork. For your current plan vendors, use a benchmark when possible. When you change a service provider, use an RFP drafted by someone qualified, with the understanding that you need sufficient responses to make the results meaningful.

NEGOTIATING WITH VENDORS

Benchmark and RFP data will equip the fiduciary committee with the needed information to negotiate with plan vendors. Having that data is like knowing the car dealer's costs before sitting down to talk about price.

Most plan vendors also have the data. They know where they stand in relation to their competition, and they know when their fees are high. If your committee determines that they are high, let your existing vendor know that you have recently conducted a benchmarking exercise and are targeting a lower fee level.

The vendor faces no liability for offering a high fee, so long as they disclose it, but you do if you accept it. I liken it to how much you pay for a seat on an airplane. Depending on the day, and the time of day, the price will differ. The airline tries to get as much money for that ticket as it can get. It's the accepted way of doing business. Some service providers for retirement plans do the same. By and large, they will charge as much as they think they can get away with for as long as they can. Only when you call them on it will they be willing to take less.

The fees are low if the total fees paid by the plan are below average when compared to plans of similar size.

Be aggressive but fair in your request. If you are a good, stable client, the vendor often will lower its fees to the 15th to 20th percentile level. If the vendor resists, make it clear that you will conduct an RFP. Often, that will result in lower fees. The vendor knows that if you do an RFP, it risks losing your business.

So how can the committee be confident that the plan's fees are low? The fees are low if the total fees paid by the plan are below average when compared to plans of similar size. This can be calculated by totaling the fees paid to each plan service or service provider and comparing it to the total of the average (50th percentile) benchmark fees. Remember not to count investment-related fees that are deducted from the returns for the investment lineup performance test. To do so would be double counting them.

BE WARY OF INDIVIDUAL ADVICE PROGRAMS

As the opening story in this chapter illustrated, individual advice services for participants can be very costly—and yet they are on the rise, being peddled by plan advisers and recordkeepers. They have discovered that it is easy to sell to participants who are clamoring for help when deciding how to invest their money. Fiduciary committees frequently approve such a program with the idea that each participant can make his or her own decision about its merits. At the same time, many participants believe that the employer has endorsed it.

That combination—the participants wanting help, the committee not scrutinizing the advice program, and the participants thinking the employer endorses it—has led to large and unchecked plan expenses.

The participant advice programs, in general, work like this: The participant speaks with an adviser or representative. The participant gives an expected retirement date; takes an assessment of risk tolerance; and details current plan assets, any other retirement assets, and expected annual contributions, among other things. The meeting usually lasts thirty minutes to an hour.

After the information is collected, the adviser uses a software program to recommend a custom portfolio for the participant among the plan's investment menu. Typically, the portfolio will be rebalanced periodically and gradually reallocated to a more conservative posture as the participant grows older.

In most ways, the participant advice program works similarly to a target date fund (TDF). The main difference is that the TDF doesn't take into account the individual risk tolerance of the participant and doesn't consider the effect of any outside assets on its allocation. The participant's account in a TDF is managed just like everyone else's in the fund who expects to retire at about the same time.

The service may be valuable for circumstances where a participant has a very low or high risk tolerance or where the participant has large assets outside of the plan. For most participants, however, the advice program will work very much like a TDF.

The fee for providing that advice service to participants can be substantial. The total charge often will be an asset-based fee of 0.25 percent to 0.75 percent a year or even higher. That is on top of the expenses charged by the individual funds. As you saw earlier, fees of this amount will dramatically reduce the amount of money ultimately accumulated for retirement. And the performance of the custom advice isn't monitored by the committee because it is provided individually. The participant also doesn't typically monitor the performance through benchmarking or other measures because the individual often isn't a sophisticated investor. So, the expense is certain but the value is unknown. In my experience, when there is little incentive for the adviser to deliver performance, it has nearly always meant that the performance is bad.

Furthermore, those who sell the program also often conduct the enrollment meetings, encouraging people to sign up for the added service (and the added fees). When the salesperson for the advice program also conducts the enrollment meetings, it isn't unusual to see adoption by 80 percent or more of participants. I have seen that happen many times.

Far better in my opinion to pay an hourly rate to a fee-only financial planner who is dedicated to serving the client's interests exclusively. To pay, say, $500 just once is very inexpensive when compared to paying an asset-based advice fee each and every year.

The fiduciary committee has a duty to prudently select and monitor the advice program, so be cautious when considering it. Again, keep in mind that many of the participants will put a lot of faith in what they see as a program endorsed by their employer. Be mindful of the total charges to the plan. If the adviser charges an asset-based fee, be wary.

Investment advice services to participants are not yet all that prevalent in the industry, but the investment and plan adviser industries are targeting them aggressively. A few bad actors out there have done substantial harm to employee accounts. I would like to see new regulations end the abuses. Frankly, though, it's more likely to end when enough participants wise up to the abuse, file legal action, and prevail in court.

WHY STOP AT REASONABLE?

Since ERISA 408(b)(2) establishes a reasonable standard for vendor compensation, many fiduciary committees will adhere closely to that direction as they examine their own plan fees. That is a rational and defensible position, but is it the best you can do? Could you get lower than reasonable?

Price isn't everything, of course. Quality and performance also are important factors to consider. But all things being equal, the price that the plan pays for services matters a great deal. Therefore, think of reasonable as the starting line, not the finish line.

Remember, every dollar saved in plan expenses is the equivalent to putting a dollar in the participant's accounts to grow through the years. As a plan fiduciary, you have no control over how the financial markets will perform. You do have control over the services provided to the plan and the expenses that your plan pays.

THE BOTTOM LINE

- Expenses paid by the plan are essentially a negative return for the participants.
- A good way to lower your plan's fees is to ask the employer to pay some or all of them.
- Your committee can better negotiate a lower fee by getting information about costs of the service beforehand, via a benchmark or an RFP.
- Independent, third-party benchmarks are the most reliable. RFPs are more reliable when they get many responses and experts write them.
- Try to do better than "reasonable" in pushing for lower plan expenses.
- Plan fees are low when the total fees paid by the plan are below average when compared to plans of similar size.

CHAPTER 8

CONTRIBUTIONS MATTER MOST

At this point, you have learned a great deal about serving as a fiduciary committee member of an employer-sponsored retirement plan. You want to do a good job. You take the role seriously and want to see your company's employees put on track for retirement and build financial security for themselves along the way. It's clear to you now that the difference between providing a good plan and a not-so-good plan will have a big impact on their success. It is a big responsibility, but one that also allows you to make a real difference in people's lives and the lives of their families and communities.

Now that you are knowledgeable and motivated, I must tell you something else: it might not matter. Why? Because success depends on the contributions put into the plan. Perfect oversight and management can't overcome no or low contributions.

To be completely clear, there isn't even a fiduciary duty to get employees to contribute to the plan. You have no such obligation legally. As a result, many employers will take the position that employees can take it or leave it. "Here it is. If you want to use it, use it. If you don't, don't. That is up to you." Fiduciary committees must still manage the plan in the best interests of its participants. But the amount the participants contribute, or whether they contribute or not, isn't your concern—legally.

If you, your committee, or your company has that attitude, then you don't need to read this chapter. You can skip ahead to the conclusion. If, on the other hand, you and your company believe that putting as many people as possible on a path to retirement is socially responsible, beneficial for them and the company, this chapter is critically important. In the pages ahead, you will learn the best way to get more contributions into the plan. You will discover how to know whether those contributions are at a level where you can be confident that your plan is functioning true to its aim.

THE MOST IMPORTANT QUESTION

Many financial planners suggest that the typical retired American will need 70 to 80 percent of his or her preretirement income to maintain a similar standard of living. That's where the rubber meets the road. Will enough money be coming in every month to support the retiree's accustomed lifestyle? Some will need more than 80 percent, and some will do just fine on less than 70 percent, but that range is a good guide to assess how well a retirement plan is performing.

As we've seen, investment returns and plan fees are important factors in determining how much an account can grow over a working career. But their impact pales in comparison to how much money the participants put into the plan. Strong returns and low expenses cannot make up for insufficient contributions. The biggest factor in account growth isn't the investment returns or the plan fees. It's how much the participants set aside from their paychecks.

The recommended contribution percentage for the average American worker is generally between 10 to 20 percent of income per year. The amount varies due to several factors, chief of which is how early the worker starts saving for retirement. As seen in the charts here, a person who contributes 10 percent beginning at age twenty-four and continues at that pace is likely to be in good shape by his or her late sixties. Those who wait until their early forties need to contribute a higher percentage to get similar results.

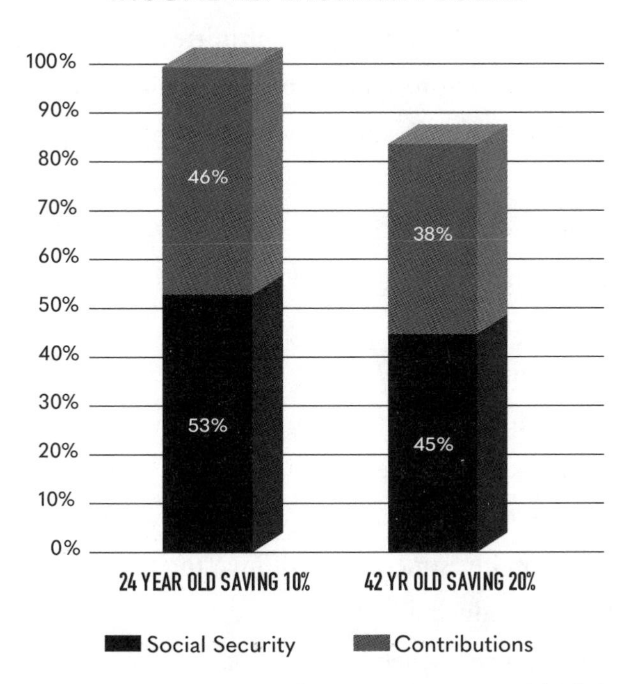

This assumes a retirement age of sixty-seven, income of $44k for the forty-two-year-old and $30.8k for the twenty-four-year-old, a rate of return of 6 percent, inflation of 2 percent, and Social Security of 35 percent.

Therefore, it is imperative that employees contribute 10 to 20 percent of their paychecks if they are to retire successfully. Any amount that the employer contributes as a match or by other means is included in that total.

INDIVIDUAL PROGRESS IS TOUGH TO CALCULATE

To know whether someone is financially prepared for retirement, you would need to know that person's preretirement income and compare it to the income available in retirement—the income replacement percentage. Those who can replace much of their take-home pay generally will be able to retire comfortably (assuming their financial life before retirement was comfortable).

But how does the fiduciary committee know whether the employees are contributing enough money to hit the desired income replacement percentage? To approximate the percent of preretirement income that each employee will be able to replace in retirement, you would need to know or estimate the following:

- Current age
- Retirement age
- Current income
- Current retirement savings balance
- Other assets available for retirement (i.e., future inheritance)
- Total contributions per year until retirement
- Return on investments, net of investment fees
- Plan fees deducted
- Social Security benefits
- Inflation rate
- Life expectancy

Individually, your employees could use that information to project an income replacement percentage needed in retirement, thereby knowing whether they are saving enough. Your plan's recordkeeper likely has a website calculator to provide an estimate. If not, dozens of other sites have such calculators.

Your fiduciary committee, however, simply won't have all of that information for each employee. You can get much of it: current income, current contributions, and plan fees, for example. You can estimate investment returns, inflation, and life expectancy. However, each employee would have to tell you directly about any other retirement savings or available assets.

And that's the problem. You would think, with the amount of data available today, that a fiduciary committee should be able to calculate whether the employees are on track. But a few key pieces of information cannot be obtained without great effort or cost.

Meanwhile, today's workforce is more mobile than ever, as any HR department can attest. Few employees stay with a company for an entire career. A 2018 survey by the Bureau of Labor Statistics found that the typical American worker had been with his or her current employer for 4.2 years, largely unchanged from earlier surveys.[17] That translates to eight to ten employers over the course of a career—and the worker might participate in that many retirement plans, as well.

As a result, many of your plan participants will have other retirement savings scattered among various accounts. They may have money in former employers' plans. They also may have individual retirement accounts with direct contributions or rollovers from other plans. Some will have spouses with their own retirement account balances, and some may be eligible for pensions from former employers or from military or government service.

17 "Employee Tenure Survey," US Bureau of Labor Statistics, September 20, 2018, https://www.bls.gov/news.release/tenure.nr0.htm.

Ideally, your fiduciary committee would be able to calculate the income replacement status of each participant—but as you can see, that would be a challenging or impossible task.

COMMON MEASURES OF RETIREMENT READINESS

At committee meetings, you probably have seen the following common metrics that use data to try to get a general picture of the plan participants' retirement readiness. They are helpful measures, and together they are leading indicators of the projected income replacement percentage of the employees, in total.

Participation rate refers to the percentage of eligible participants who have a plan balance. A high participation rate indicates that a good portion of the workforce has money in the plan. They either are contributing currently or have contributed previously.

Average deferral rate is typically based on participants who actively are deferring part of their compensation into the plan. It quantifies the average percentage of compensation that each person in this group contributes. If you approximate the match that is associated with the average deferral rate, it is possible to get an estimate of the total contribution the average participant is receiving. This percentage can then be compared to the recommended contribution of 10 to 20 percent.

Average account balance is the total plan balance divided by the total number of eligible participants. High average account balances plus high participation rates plus high average deferral rates likely indicate that your 401(k) or 403(b) plan is successfully preparing your employees for retirement.

While each of those metrics is helpful, they also can be misleading. For example:

- While a high participation rate among the plan's eligible participants is a favorable indicator, if this is combined with low deferral rates it likely means that a high percentage of the participants are deferring a low percentage of their check each pay period.
- If the plan has high deferral rates with low levels of participation, this indicates that a relatively small percentage of the eligible participants are deferring a high percentage of their compensation each pay period. That might indicate greater participation among the more highly paid participants, with less participation by lower-paid participants.
- A low average account balance is unlikely to produce a sufficient income replacement ratio even with high participation and high deferral rates. The only exception would be if the average age of the employees is very young, since they would have time on their side. Remember, *average account balance* only measures the money in your plan. Assets that employees hold in previous employer plans or in personal savings are outside the view of the committee.

BENCHMARKING YOUR PLAN'S SUCCESS

Since you can't determine the income replacement ratio of each employee, I recommend that you base it on your average employee: Your plan's contributions are sufficient if the average eligible participant is on track to replace 70 percent or more of their income in retirement.

Revisiting the previous list, you need the following information to calculate the income replacement ratio of your average employee:

- Average age
- Assumed retirement age
- Average income
- Average account balance
- Average annual total contributions
- An assumed return on investments, net of investment fees
- An assumed amount of plan fees deducted as a percent of assets
- Projected Social Security benefits for the average income level above
- Assumed inflation rate
- Assumed life expectancy

Your plan's contributions are sufficient if the average eligible participant is on track to replace 70 percent or more of their income in retirement.

Note that you will not be able to obtain information on outside assets. Therefore, the calculation will likely underreport the true income replacement ratio of your average employee. However, you can reasonably assume that if the calculation yields a ratio of 70 percent or more, your employees generally are contributing enough to be on track for retirement.

MOVING THE NEEDLE

Once you begin benchmarking the plan's success this way, the question will turn to improving your results. How can you move the needle? Remember, the total annual plan contributions (by both the employees and the employer) are the main factor in determining the percentage of income replacement for retirement.

The best thing that the fiduciary committee can do to improve the income replacement ratio is to get the employer to adopt a properly structured automatic enrollment feature with automatic escalation. Nothing else will make as big an impact. That will require amending the plan's terms, which is an employer function. A fiduciary committee doesn't have that authority, but it can advocate for the change.

Establishing automatic provisions will require the employer to comply with provisions of the Pension Protection Act (PPA) of 2006 and subsequent regulations. Likewise, the fiduciary committee will need to make sure the plan is compliant with those rules and regulations in its operation. Be sure to seek counsel from your ERISA attorney for guidance.

The PPA was the catalyst for the growth in auto features in 401(k)s and 403(b)s. Some employers introduced auto features before the PPA, but their popularity grew dramatically afterward. The PPA and the later regulations encouraged that growth by establishing clear standards and outlining safe-harbor provisions to protect plans that adopt auto features from enforcement action. The required timing and content of employee notifications is one of those standards.

Today, about two-thirds of plans offer automatic enrollment, according to the Plan Sponsor Council of America's annual survey. In 2007, only about a third of them offered it. Employers can choose from different types of automatic enrollment features: a basic automatic contribution arrangement (ACA), an eligible automatic contribution arrangement (EACA), and a qualified automatic contribution arrangement (QACA). The sponsor's ERISA attorney can provide guidance. Let's take a closer look at how the auto features work.

AUTOMATIC ENROLLMENT

Automatic enrollment (auto-enroll) allows an employer to automatically deduct a set amount from an employee's wages unless the employee elects not to contribute or to contribute a different amount. With the traditional voluntary enrollment, newly eligible employees often don't complete the process and might stay out of the plan for years. Because they do nothing, they're out. With auto-enroll, if they do nothing, they're in. If they don't want to participate, they must say so.

As a result, auto-enroll dramatically improves participation rates. According to a 2018 Vanguard research paper, *Automatic enrollment: The power of the default*, the feature nearly doubles participation rates among new hires, from 47 percent under voluntary enrollment to 93 percent under auto-enroll.[18]

In an auto-enroll plan, employers must declare the default deferral rate (or amount) that will be automatically deducted from employee wages. That's a critical decision. A good choice will have lasting positive outcomes for the participants. A poor one will do more harm than good.

A low automatic deferral rate, say 1 to 2 percent, looks appealing to many employers who are wary of pushback from employees for taking money from their paychecks. However, if your employer adopts a low deferral rate, many, if not most, employees will be forever on a path of saving too little for retirement. Remember, the goal is 10 to

---

18 Jean Young, "Automatic enrollment: The power of the default," Vanguard, March 1, 2018, https://institutional.vanguard.com/VGApp/iip/site/institutional/researchcommentary/article/InvResPowerDefault.

20 percent of total wages. In trying to do good by adding auto-enroll, the employer instead will have harmed the retirement readiness of many employees.

An initial default deferral rate of 5 percent, combined with auto-escalation (see the next section), will typically set employees up for retirement success. Employers often ask, however, whether a higher initial rate will result in more employees dropping out of the plan. The Vanguard study addressed that question: "Our results suggest that employee quit rates do not appear to vary in response to a plan sponsor's choice of the initial contribution rate. The participation rate among employees earning less than $30,000 is around 85 percent—regardless of whether the initial contribution rate is 2 percent or 6 percent."

That initial deferral of 5 percent or more is a vital step in putting employees on the path to a successful retirement. Be prepared to advocate for the employees. Sharing that information will help your employer see why it is so important.

AUTO-ESCALATION

Auto-escalation is an add-on feature to auto-enroll. With it, the deferral rate automatically increases each year until it reaches a preset maximum. Annual increments of 1 percentage point with a 10 percent maximum are typical. Without auto-escalation, the auto-enrolled participants often fail to increase their deferral percentage over time. Inertia tends to keep them at the default rate.

For most plans, the combination of auto-enroll with auto-escalation dramatically increases the plan's participation and average deferral rate. The chart illustrates a typical 5 percent initial default rate with an annual 1 percent escalation and a 10 percent cap.

PERCENTAGE WITHHELD FROM COMPENSATION	YEAR OF PARTICIPATION IN THE PLAN
5%	1
6%	2
7%	3
8%	4
9%	5
10%	6

That arrangement will have most employees receiving a total plan contribution (including employer match) of 10 percent in just a few years. For long-term employees, those combined contributions will total 13 percent or more, depending on the match amount.

AUTO RE-ENROLLMENT

Auto re-enrollment is another option for plans with auto-enroll. It applies the default deferral rate to existing eligible participants who are deferring below a threshold amount. The intent is to bring them up to speed.

Here's how it works:

- The decision is made to conduct a re-enrollment at the default deferral—let's say 5 percent.
- Next, it is decided to re-enroll eligible participants who are currently below a threshold level—let's say those deferring 3 percent or less.
- Finally, the effective date (say, Jan. 1) is decided. On that date, all eligible participants who are deferring 3 percent or

less, and who don't opt out of the change, will automatically begin deferring 5 percent.

Auto re-enroll can make a dramatic impact on plans that have low participation or low average deferral rates. In one fell swoop, hundreds or thousands of eligible participants can be set on an appropriate path for retirement. Initially, some ERISA attorneys weren't sure about auto re-enroll because the PPA doesn't specifically mention it or provide a safe harbor for it. However, its popularity has grown dramatically since then as employers and fiduciaries look to increase retirement readiness.

Default Investment Option

If your employer adopts an automatic contribution arrangement, the fiduciary committee will need to select a qualified default investment alternative (QDIA). The QDIA is an investment option where contributions are sent if the participant has not provided direction—and when a plan has auto features, most of the new enrollees won't immediately select a fund. They might do so later after they begin getting statements, but their initial contributions will typically go into the default option.

The Department of Labor issued a regulation under the PPA that gives fiduciaries safe-harbor relief from fiduciary liability for investment outcomes if they comply with the appropriate QDIA provisions. In an April 2008 fact sheet, the department's Employee Benefits Security Administration stated that a QDIA must meet, among other things, the following conditions:

- Participants and beneficiaries must have been given an opportunity to provide investment direction but have not done so.
- A notice generally must be furnished to participants and beneficiaries in advance of the first investment in the QDIA and

annually thereafter. The rule describes the information that must be included in the notice.

- Materials such as investment prospectuses that are provided to the plan for the QDIA must be furnished to participants and beneficiaries.
- Participants and beneficiaries must have the opportunity to direct investments out of a QDIA as frequently as from other plan investments, but at least quarterly.
- The rule limits the fees that can be imposed on participants who opt out of the plan or who decide to direct their investments.
- The plan must offer a "broad range of investment alternatives" as defined in the department's regulation under Section 404(c) of ERISA.
- The final regulation does not absolve fiduciaries of the duty to prudently select and monitor QDIAs.
- The final regulation provides for four types of QDIAs:
    - A product with a mix of investments that takes into account the individual's age or retirement date (an example of such a product could be a lifecycle or target date fund).
    - An investment service that allocates contributions among existing plan options to provide an asset mix that takes into account the individual's age or retirement date (an example of such a service could be a professionally managed account [i.e., individualized advice program]).

  - A product with a mix of investments that takes into account the characteristics of the group of employees as a whole, rather than each individual (an example of such a product could be a balanced fund).
  - A capital preservation product for only the first one hundred twenty days of participation (an option for plan sponsors wishing to simplify administration if workers opt out of participation before incurring an additional tax).

- A QDIA must be managed by either an investment manager, plan trustee, plan sponsor, or a committee composed primarily of employees of the plan sponsor that is a named fiduciary, or be an investment company registered under the Investment Company Act of 1940.
- A QDIA generally may not invest participant contributions in employer securities.

TDFs are the predominant choice of fiduciary committees for QDIAs. These are diversified funds in which the investment mix is based on the participant's expected retirement date. Whatever your choice, you will want your ERISA attorney to confirm that it meets the requirements of the regulation.

ADVISER-LED EDUCATION MEETINGS

If your employer won't adopt auto features or if your plan's auto features aren't resulting in enough contributions into the plan, your committee may choose to pay an adviser to conduct educational meetings for your participants.

For plans without auto-enroll, an adviser is commonly hired to conduct group enrollment meetings or one-on-one meetings with each newly eligible participant. The adviser often has more knowledge than the HR or benefits staff about the investment options and assists the new participants with the enrollment process, including help with choosing from the investment menu.

An effective adviser can influence new participants to contribute a higher amount by explaining how the choice influences their future retirement savings. Over time, more participants deferring more money will begin to increase the participation rates, average deferral rates, and average account balances. These, in turn, increase the projected income replacement ratio of your average employee.

The downside is that the adviser comes with a cost that is typically paid by the plan. At a large organization, paying an adviser to meet with each new participant becomes very expensive. That expense is paid by all the plan's participants, not just the newly eligible ones who meet with them.

If you employ an adviser to conduct enrollment meetings, be sure to measure the value to the plan. What did the plan get for the money? In each time period, how much value did the adviser provide by increasing the projected income replacement ratios, as compared with the expense to the plan? Also, make sure the adviser isn't selling other services to the participants, such as those continuing advice services for additional fees. As mentioned earlier, employees will tend to view advisers who meet with them as endorsed by the employer. For that reason, the employees will likely accept a sales pitch for additional services.

LET'S GO AUTO

Automatic contribution arrangements have proved to be much more effective at driving income replacement ratios than adviser-led enrollment meetings. From the employer's perspective, however, the auto features can raise two concerns:

1. Will the employees resent the paternalistic approach?
2. Will providing the match get costly if participation rates rise dramatically?

From your perspective as a plan fiduciary, auto-enroll with auto-escalation is the best deal. It is the most effective way to get participants saving enough to be on track for retirement—and it doesn't cost the plan anything. If the employer adds those features, then enrollment by the adviser certainly isn't necessary, and the plan saves the cost of having the adviser conduct those meetings.

So how can you get your employer to see the light? Explain the benefits all around. Not only will the employees be preparing for a more fulfilling retirement, but their increased financial security will make them more productive at work. And they will be able to afford to retire on time, meaning they will free up spots for younger people who will come in at a lower salary and likely stick around longer because they see room for advancement. When an employer sees that what helps the workforce also helps the organization do well, good things happen.

Automatic contribution arrangements have proved to be much more effective at driving income replacement ratios than adviser-led enrollment meetings.

THE BOTTOM LINE

- The goal of a retirement plan is to give participants the ability to retire comfortably. You can measure whether your plan is succeeding in doing that.
- To gauge contribution amounts, look at the projected income replacement ratio of an average eligible participant.
- Auto-enrollment and auto-escalation are the most effective ways to increase contributions and improve income replacement ratios.
- Automatic enrollment should be set at a default deferral rate of 5 percent or more, with automatic escalation of 1 percent annually to a cap of no less than 10 percent.
- The plan's contributions are sufficient if the average eligible participant is on track to replace 70 percent or more of their income in retirement.

CONCLUSION

DOING WELL BY DOING GOOD

Financial insecurity has long been rampant in our nation. Even workers with supposedly good jobs often lack a sense of financial confidence beyond the next paycheck. They know they should be saving for retirement. Many are not. The stress reverberates through their family, their community, and our society. It's hard to be happy and productive when you don't know what tomorrow may bring.

The rise of the 401(k) and 403(b) plans has the potential to make a major difference. Countless people who otherwise would not be saving a cent for retirement are now anticipating their retirement as a time of dreams, not drudgery. As their accounts grow, so does their hope.

Those retirement plans are governed by laws and regulations that have evolved through the decades to address a long history of pension abuse. They have helped but haven't eliminated it. Without a watchdog to look out for the participants in those plans, their retirement dreams could be dashed.

As a member of your plan's fiduciary committee, you are that watchdog. You are also their advocate who will stand up for their interests when others might try to take advantage of them. You are doing far more than assessing funds and fees to make sure your plan is a strong one for your fellow employees. You also are changing our society.

Across the nation, millions of people are serving just like you on fiduciary committees for organizations large and small. My wish is for each of those servants to become empowered to make a difference in the lives of the participants of their plans. Let's walk through the essence of what has been covered.

A well-functioning retirement plan benefits both the employees and the employer. It sets the employees on course to a fruitful retirement, relieving them of the stress of financial uncertainty and boosting their productivity during their working years. When workers do retire as planned, they often open spots in the workplace for younger employees with new perspectives who come in lower on the pay scale.

A well-functioning retirement plan benefits both the employees and the employer.

The fiduciary committee members, who serve solely in the interests of the participants and beneficiaries, need not wonder whether their organization's plan is a good one and whether they are managing it properly. They can know for sure by measuring it against objective standards. Good plans have these three characteristics: the investment lineup performs well, fees are low, and participant contributions are at a sufficient amount.

Employees today can plan more confidently for retirement thanks to a body of federal laws and regulations collectively known as ERISA (the Employee Retirement Income Security Act of 1974), which was the original legislation designed to curtail pension plan abuses. The 1974 act often has been amended, particularly to accommodate the rise of the defined-contribution plans that, since the 1980s, have replaced many of the defined-benefit pension plans.

With these newer and ubiquitous 401(k)-style plans, employees now can choose their own investment funds, whether or not they know anything about the markets at all. ERISA established fiduciary standards seeking to inform and protect the plan participants. The Department of Labor and Internal Revenue Service are the primary agencies that enforce ERISA.

The employer, when establishing a retirement plan, sets its terms and conditions. Those rules, such as the vesting schedule and the amount of an employer match, vary from plan to plan. Many of the plan's terms must meet minimum ERISA standards, however. The employer can choose the rules with business interests in mind. However, the fiduciary committee must serve only the best interests of the participants. It must not make decisions based on what would be best for the organization. The committee can spend plan assets to manage the plan, but the employer, with few exceptions, must keep hands off.

The governing provisions of a plan are set forth in a comprehensive legal document and in a shorter Summary Plan Description, which is written in plain language. The SPD is the document provided to participants and beneficiaries to inform them of the plan's benefits and other provisions. Any amendments to the plan must be reflected in both those documents. The fiduciaries must be alert to such changes and make sure the internal staff is observing them. Failure to follow the rules can lead to severe consequences.

Those consequences come in two varieties: federal enforcement action and lawsuits. If a plan's management fails to comply with ERISA standards, it could face fines and penalties as severe as disqualification, although the DOL and IRS allow for corrective measures. Lawsuits are the bigger financial threat to fiduciaries and plan sponsors and have become increasingly common, most often accusing them of allowing excessive fees, offering inappropriate investment choices, and self-dealing.

Fiduciary committee members typically are included as a target of the lawsuits. As a condition of serving, they should insist on either fiduciary liability insurance or written indemnification from the employer. The committee should hire an attorney who specializes in ERISA and agrees to serve its interests. The committee also should conduct its business formally and keep thorough minutes that document the process used to make decisions.

Hiring the service providers is a key function of the fiduciary committee. The committee must make sure that those providers are charging reasonable fees for necessary services. They generally include the plan adviser, recordkeeper, custodian, ERISA attorney, and plan auditor. The committee also must oversee the internal staff members who handle the day-to-day details of operating the plan.

The plan adviser is a particularly crucial choice and will have much to do with how well the plan performs. However, conflicts of interest are appallingly common. Investment companies often woo plan advisers with trips, gifts, or marketing assistance to get the advisers to recommend their products. A plan adviser should give the committee written acceptance of fiduciary responsibility, either as a

3(21) adviser who recommends funds for the committee to choose or as a 3(38) manager who has discretion to design the fund menu.

That choice of funds, known as manager selection, is critical because it will translate into how well the investment lineup performs and therefore how well each participant's portfolio performs. Compounded over a working career, even a slight improvement in that performance can make a dramatic difference in the assets available for retirement.

To properly determine how your investment lineup has performed, you should first measure the performance of each fund against an index that tracks the same asset class of the fund. Don't be lulled into continuing to look at a fund's track record before it was added to the lineup. What matters is how well it performs during the time that it is available to participants. That is what will influence their accounts, and that's also the true measure of the plan adviser's value. *You will know an investment lineup is performing well when it outperforms an all-index lineup, net of investment-related fees.*

The plan adviser also plays a key role in recommending other service providers and helping the fiduciary committee negotiate and monitor their fees. Because those fees usually are paid from plan assets, they reduce the amount of money available to invest and therefore slow the growth of each participant's account. Even if a fee cuts the rate of return by only a fraction of a percentage point, that loss compounds negatively and can dramatically reduce the participant's nest egg at retirement.

The fiduciary committee can know *the fees are low if they are less than what plans of similar size are paying on average.* The way to find out is to obtain an independent, third-party benchmark for each service, which the committee can also use for leverage when negotiating with potential providers. If necessary, the committee also can conduct an RFP to seek information on services and fees specific to the plan from a variety of providers.

What matters more than fees and investment performance, however, is the amount that plan participants contribute regularly from their paychecks. If they aren't setting aside enough money, they won't attain much growth—no matter how low the fees or how strong the funds they choose. It's not a fiduciary duty to ensure that employees are saving sufficiently, but a good plan nonetheless keeps them on track to retire on time.

No need to speculate about that, however. How well a plan is succeeding can be measured. With so many variables, it's next to impossible to know whether any individual is on track; however, it certainly is possible to assess whether the participants *on average* are contributing enough so that they are likely to retire without compromising their standard of living.

The best way to promote the necessary level of savings is to institute an automatic enrollment and escalation feature. My recommendation is to start at a default deferral of 5 percent or more of compensation and increase by 1 point annually to at least 10 percent. You can be confident that *the necessary contributions are being made if the average eligible participant is on track to replace 70 percent of their preretirement income in retirement.*

Your work is both a challenge and an honor. As a retirement plan fiduciary, you have been chosen to serve for an important cause. You are an ambassador for your colleagues in the workplace who are depending on you to speak out for them as they work their way toward a rewarding retirement. As they thrive, so will their families and their communities. All benefit from your vigilance as you demonstrate the truth of the old saying "doing well by doing good." Your mission is nothing less than helping people succeed. If they do, so have you.

ACKNOWLEDGMENTS

The idea for this book first hit me in the fall of 2018. Soon after, I reached out to Roger Wohlner. Roger is a practicing financial planner in the Chicago area and is a freelance writer. He was generous with his time and gave me invaluable feedback on how the process might unfold.

Cody Mendenhall was the next person that I approached. He is the executive director of Pension Consultants. I've worked with Cody for many years. He encouraged me to pursue it. Without him giving me encouragement at that early stage, I would not have continued. I am grateful to be his colleague and friend, and I'm indebted to him for his guidance.

Over the next six months, I worked to develop an outline and began writing with Roger. He and I worked very closely together to create the first manuscript. At each step, Roger was upbeat and took on the role of coach—even as I made countless changes. He was always very patient with me.

With the initial manuscript completed, I contacted Advantage Media Group, who agreed to publish it. However, the original manuscript would need to be further developed. By the end, its volume grew by 50 percent.

Along the way, I solicited several in the office to read drafts of chapters to help with clarity and accuracy. Cody generously read the entire manuscript several times and offered me valuable feedback. Jarod Robilard, manager of our RetireAdvisers team, read the chapter on contributions and helped me with calculations that led to several charts in the book. Jarod was always eager to help and quick to reply. I am thankful for his expertise and his kindness. I asked Dave Clemenson, Vendor Services Consultant, to read the chapter on fees and give me his thoughts. He was generous and quick to respond. Dave is one of the most thorough, detailed people I have ever worked with. He is also professional, kind, and thoughtful. Chris Thixton, who has been my partner for twenty-five years, read several chapters. Chris is a trusted partner and friend. I value his input and trust his judgment. He gave me good insight on how to clarify certain sections to make it easier to understand. Lisa Goyer (in-house ERISA attorney) was my go-to for ERISA technical issues. She was gracious to read the chapters that had substantial references to laws and regulations. She alerted me to potential misstatements. Later, Lisa went through the entire manuscript with me. Throughout it all, she was smart, observant, and patient. Her expertise and advice gave me the confidence I needed to complete the book. Mary Sue Hoban, our marketing manager, also read the entire manuscript. Mary Sue is detail oriented. She would make a superb editor. She gave me great feedback on wording, grammar (of which I sometimes struggle), and syntax. I am grateful for her eagle eye and thoughtfulness.

This book also required a review from our compliance team. Jenna Pfeifer, chief compliance officer, and Liz Nemeti, compliance specialist, spent many hours reviewing draft copies and told me where I needed disclaimers and disclosures. It was their job to make sure I didn't run afoul of any SEC rules. They were very thorough, detailed, and yet kind. They are outstanding professionals. I am thankful for their expertise.

My team at Advantage Media Group has guided me every step of the way. Robert (Bob) Sheasley worked closely with me on development and flow. Nate Best has been my editor and Kristin Goodale my project manager. I have relied on them continuously and they have been great to work with. Without them, the book simply wouldn't have been possible.

The finished product has been a team effort. I am forever grateful and indebted to you all.